FROM THE ROOTS UP

Economic Development

as if Community Mattered

David P. Ross

and

Peter J. Usher

with a Foreword by George McRobie

The Bootstrap Press

Croton-on-Hudson, New York

Published in cooperation with the Vanier Institute of the Family, Ottawa, by The Bootstrap Press, an imprint of the Intermediate Technology Development Group of North America, Inc., P.O. Box 337, Croton-on-Hudson, New York 10520

Library of Congress Cataloging-in-Publication Data

Ross, David P.
   From the roots up.

   Bibliography: p.
   1. Informal sector (Economics) 2. Economic development--Social aspects. I. Usher, Peter J. II. Title.
HD2341.R66 1986   338.9   85-27972
ISBN 0-942850-04-1

Printed in the United States of America

TABLE OF CONTENTS

iii

iv

FOREWORD

The new economists will set about invent-
ing new criteria of efficiency, practicality
and economic reality that will be grounded
in the vocational needs of people.

Theodore Roszak

In the mid-1960s, the conventional wisdom of economic development was informed by the notion that cheap and abundant energy and rapid technological progress had opened up an era of limitless economic growth. Few questioned either the survival value--the sustainability--of an industrial system, based firmly on the heedless exploitation of people and finite natural resources, or the wisdom of advocating its universal adoption, especially by poor people in poor countries.

Today, 20 years on, it is no longer a tiny minority who are convinced that the particular kind of industrialization pursued by the rich countries is not sustainable; that there is not the remotest possibility of its universal adoption (fortunately, one might add, for the future of mankind); and that the Third World, instead of modeling its development on that of the North, should unhook itself from its dependence upon the rich industrialized countries as quickly as possible.

The reasons why conventional industrialization has increasingly come to be recognized as a self-defeating system are familiar enough. There is, first, its almost total dependence on non-renewable resources, especially oil. The price and the

vii

availability of oil are by now familiar sources of international tension. The industrialized countries are in the unenviable position of the businessman who has confused capital with income --a practice that often leads to jail--and who has limited power over those who supply his capital.

Secondly, the North's pattern and character of industrialization is on a collision course with the natural environment. The pollution of groundwater and food by industrial and agro-chemicals; acid rain; the appalling prospect of accumulating what are, for all practical purposes, permanently lethal radioactive wastes; the destruction of forests and the erosion of arable land; the threat of climatic change arising from the "greenhouse effect" of accumulating carbon dioxide in the atmosphere--all these are some of the danger signals that have become visible in the past two decades, and what they are signaling is that in and around at least the industrialized countries, mankind is on the way to becoming an endangered species.

On the grounds of resource and environmental conservation alone then, the search should be on for technologies, ways of producing necessary goods and services, that are more sparing in their use of non-renewable resources, and as far as humanly possible, non-violent towards the living environment. "We speak of the battle with Nature," Fritz Schumacher once said, "But we would do well to remember that if we win that battle, we are on the losing side."

Thanks to the work of the growing network of appropriate technology organizations around the world, we already have some idea of the kinds of technology that can be produced when engineers turn their minds to saving capital and energy instead of labor. They are mostly small-scale, such as a cement plant which produces about one-hundredth the output of a conventional large-scale plant or a sugar mill which is one-fortieth the capital cost of a big mill. This means that they can utilize local raw materials and serve local markets, eliminating long transport hauls while providing work for local people. In other instances, small-scale units may operate on a seasonal basis, fitting in with the seasonal patterns of agriculture. Renewable energy systems using non-polluting energy sources such as the sun, the wind and water, are by their nature decentralized. It is no longer a matter of speculation but of fact that efficient, small-scale technologies can be devised to suit a wide variety of local needs and resources.

There is a third reason for the rapidly growing disenchantment with conventional industrialization. This is its pervasive tendency to "eliminate the human factor" or more simply to create unemployment. Official rates of unemployment (which in varying degrees understate the size of the problem) were ranging between 10 and 15 percent in the industrialized countries on both sides of the Atlantic in the mid-1980s; localized unemployment, within countries, is often as high as 20 percent of more, and it is also particularly high among the young.

The curse of high and growing joblessness in the face of a multitude of unmet needs is, of course, a long-standing problem for the Third World, so I will approach the subject through the Third World's experience of industrialization.

Few things have been more clearly demonstrated during the past 20 years than the fact that the conventional industrial technologies of the rich countries, technologies that are typically large-scale, very expensive, labor-saving and capital- and energy-intensive, have nothing positive to offer the great majority of poor people in the Third World. There is evidence, indeed, to suggest that large-scale, city-centered technologies compete out of existence what few non-farm activities there are in the rural areas. The Third World's almost total reliance upon the rich-country technologies has resulted in a grotesquely lopsided and inequitable form of development, which enriches an elite minority but bypasses the rural and urban poor--who comprise the great majority of people on the face of the earth. Virtually in total disregard of the appropriate technology movement, which has opened up real prospects for an alternative mode of development that addresses the needs and resources of the rural and urban poor, the great bulk of "development" passing from the rich countries to the Third World embodies technologies singularly inappropriate to the task of creating the millions of new workplaces through which the poor can work themselves out of their poverty. The Third World countries are now crushed by a burden of indebtedness through buying the expensive and inappropriate hardware which the rich countries find it convenient and profitable to sell to them. The impossibility of servicing these debts currently threatens a breakdown of the international monetary system.

It is hardly surprising that Third World development policies modeled on the economic systems and technologies of the rich countries have failed to improve the condition of the rural and urban poor. The life-support systems of the poor are traditional--based on family and community--and economic activity is always small scale, with barter and subsistence playing a major role. In other words, the great majority of people in poor countries live in and by the informal economy, as distinct from the formal or commercial economy. And this is precisely the sector of the economy that is ignored by policy makers and economists in the industrialized countries. Accordingly, the idea that development starts with people and what they are trying to do, and helping them to do it better--strengthening the informal economy rather than eliminating it--is unlikely to be the major motivation of industrial countries in their dealings with the Third World.

Within the industrialized countries, for the past 25 years the corporate commercial sector has been seen as the sole vehicle of economic and social progress. While the notion of limitless growth prevailed it was possible to regard the informal economy as marginal, even dispensable, and to point approvingly to the fact that many things that people used to do for themselves and for each other were being transferred to the commercial sector. Only give us growth, the argument ran (and in some quarters still runs) reflected in an ever-growing Gross National Product, and everything else will fall into place: at home, full employment, higher living standards, distributive justice, welfare, health and education; and abroad, development based on the "trickle down" theory derived from this model.

This illustration has now been dispelled. An ever-expanding conventional industrialization cannot be sustained in the face of accelerating environmental destruction and resource depletion. Nor can the Third World rely (as if it ever really could) on such continuous expansion in the North to provide expanding markets and an increasing flow of development funds. Above all, here and now, is the realization that for the industrialized countries themselves, conventional industrialization is incapable of sustaining full employment or anything like it.

Could the preoccupation with labor-saving technology be expected to provide any other result? After all, the predominant economic system in the North--not even excluding the Soviet bloc--is designed to promote the most efficient possible system of production and consumption--a system in which people fit in, if at all, as one of the factors of production, along with land and capital. The objective is not to make people more productive, creative and self-reliant and to strengthen the support systems of family and community. It is to maximize the difference between costs and revenues, and labor is a cost to be minimized and if possible eliminated altogether. Now, and as far ahead as anyone can see, we have the prospect of lower or nil rates of GNP-defined economic growth, but a continuation (indeed acceleration, in the interests of international competitiveness) of the development of labor-saving technologies. High and probably rising rates of unemployment are the common experience of the industrial countries. By and large, any feasible increases in economic growth can be produced without employing significantly more people.

If high and persistent unemployment is now characteristic of the industrialized economies, then it is of the utmost importance that informed public opinion should address itself to the implications, and more especially to practical alternative economic and social policies that could steer us off this disastrous course.

The essential and critical role of the informal economy in industrial societies has, as I have said, been both overshadowed and progressively eroded by the fully commercialized part of the economy. It is greatly to the credit of the Vanier Institute that they have never lost sight of the family and its surrounding informal sector as the very foundation of society. I would add that it is even more to their credit that they commissioned David Ross and Peter Usher to write this timely, authoritative and original book about the present and potential significance of the informal economy.

The authors are two outstanding young Canadians--one an economist; the other a geographer, of a decidedly practical bent. They set out to analyze, measure and describe the characteristics of the informal economy, contrast it with the fully commercialized sector in terms of purpose and social function, and suggest the kind of changes in economic policy that would enable the informal economy to offer new kinds of work, to strengthen local self-reliance and to meet a wide variety of economic and social needs at the local community level.

Early on the authors give a masterly summary of the predominant conventional schools of economic thought, the policies based on them and their practical consequences. They observe that neither the political right, or the left, has anything

xi

to offer by way of policies that would enable people as individuals, families and communities to become more productive, creative or self-reliant. While proclaiming the fundamental differences between (at the extremes of right and left) capitalism and communism, both sides still equate progress with ever greater industrialization and "rationalized" production of goods and delivery of services. The end results in practice look unpleasantly similar: an increasingly centralized and authoritarian economy, and an increasingly helpless and dependent public. Both right and left would squeeze out the informal economy: the one through the operation of the so-called free market--which, as Galbraith has decisively hammered home, is in fact a market tightly controlled by and in the interests of large-scale corporate enterprise--the other, through direct controls and the creation of equally large, powerful and remote bureaucracies. Yet, the informal sector is the only remaining part of modern industrial society which embodies and makes real the values that make life worth living--the values of family and community, cooperation, friendship, sharing, creativity and self-reliance. In short, the only environment in which economics can have a truly human face!

What would the informal economy amount to if one were to put a money value on its output? Taking this to be the economy of the household, the self-employed, local businesses, cooperatives of different kinds, collectives, community enterprises and a range of voluntary activities, its annual output could be valued roughly as 50 percent of the current Canadian national income. There is no reason to believe that it would be much different in other industrialized countries in the Western tradition.

But the real value of the activities within the informal economy lies precisely in the fact that they do not lend themselves to evaluation by the narrow economic calculus of commercial accounting. This is because the objectives of the two economies, the formal (or fully commercialized) and the informal, are different.

The objective of formal or conventional economic activity is, briefly, profit maximization. The essential and distinguishing characteristic of informal economic activity is that economic decisions--what to produce, where, how and for whom--are made only after weighing the human consequences: the needs of the producers, the consumers and the local community. The objectives are wider than simply maximizing financial profit. To take a simpler example, a workers' cooperative will cut profits to the bone rather than put, say, half its members out of work--its objective is not to maximize profits but to provide productive work for its members and useful product or service for the community. Or take a community enterprise which could easily make a 20 percent return on capital by investing it in the London property market. But it will always opt for a 10 or 5 percent return, or less, if by so doing it can employ, for example, some youngsters locally. The narrow economic calculus is inadequate as a measure of the human consequences of economic activity. This ability to use "social accounting," as the authors call it, rather than commercial accounting in deciding on the scale and nature of economic activity is one of the hallmarks of the informal economy. The nature of social and commercial accounting, their different implications for economic activity--what, how, for whom and why goods and services are produced--and the consequences of shifting more economic activity into the informal sector of the economy are some of the many valuable insights and analyses contained in this book.

The other distinguishing feature of informal economic activity is its small scale. Households, small businesses, community enterprises and local voluntary groups are the repositories of local self-reliance and decentralized decision making. Historically, in all industrial societies the move has been towards large scale, towards giantism in the private and public sectors and towards commercial accounting. The basic argument of this book is that if we are to restore some balance to our economies, widen opportunities for useful and productive work and arrest the trend towards authoritarianism in economic activity and in politics, we stand in need of policies deliberately designed to promote the small-scale economic activities and the social accounting that are embodied in the informal economy.

It is my belief that this book is one of the most important sequels to Fritz Schumacher's *Small is Beautiful* that has yet appeared. It draws its inspiration and illustrates its arguments from Canada, but unquestionably its message is international.

George McRobie, Co-founder of Intermediate
Technology Development Group, London,
and author of *Small is Possible*

xiii

PREFACE

With the publication of *From the Roots Up*, the Vanier Institute of the Family is pleased to introduce the work of Dr. David Ross and Dr. Peter Usher who have pursued an analysis of "economic development as if community mattered." In this book, they remind us that in the midst of all the abstract and inconclusive debates about the limitations and potentials of modern economies, it is still the original meaning of the word economy--the ordering of the household--that needs to be recalled today. As the authors make clear, we have moved too far beyond this original appreciation of the essential relationship that exists necessarily between families and communities as economically productive and the more obvious preoccupations of economists with employment, wages, inflation, trade, competitiveness, land, capital, productivity and so on and so forth. It is time to remember and to value again the informal foundation upon which the complex array of factors known to formal economic analysis are built.

The work of Ross and Usher has proceeded on the basis of the Vanier Institute's earlier studies and analyses of the informal and largely non-monetized forms of economic productivity and exchange that are pursued in homes and communities. Their contribution to a reappraisal of the narrow focus of conventional economic analysis which, by and large, excludes the informal domains of production will prove invaluable as people and their governments strive to resolve the current dilemmas of industrialized economies.

Ross and Usher have contributed to the development of the Vanier Institute's own appreciation of the place of families in modern economies for they have drawn attention to the dynamic interrelationship between the operation of the formal and informal domains that together comprise the whole economy. In this way, they have confirmed the Institute's long-standing recognition that the family cannot be adequately understood, let alone appreciated, when thought of as an isolated and discrete social unit. It is only when families are understood in their relations to changes taking place in such areas as communications, the law, technology, education, health and so on that, as a society, we will come to ask not only about the place of families in the economy but, more importantly, about the place of the economy in the lives of families and communities.

The Vanier Institute of the Family acknowledges, with thanks, the Molson Foundation which has provided the Institute with the resources that have supported the collaboration of Dr. Ross and Dr. Usher.

Vanier Institute
of the Family

ACKNOWLEDGEMENTS

As a result of attending a 1979 VIF-sponsored international seminar in Saskatchewan on the informal economy, the two authors first met and began their collaboration. We owe a debt to Bill Dyson, then the executive director of the VIF, for bringing us together to work on what has eventually become this book. As a result, the two of us worked as part-time socio-economic consultants at the Vanier Institute from 1980 to 1983, during which time (among other things) we worked on this project. We are, therefore, particularly grateful to the Institute for funding and otherwise supporting our work.

In the early stages, we had the benefit of the views of a small advisory group convened by the VIF, of whom several commented on various drafts of the book. Chief among them were Doris Badir, Arthur Cordell, Narasim Katary, Greg MacLeod, Harry Penny, Pat Reid and Andy Wells. We thank Bob Glossop, Alan Mirabelli and Ron Verzuh of the VIF for their critical review of various drafts, as well as frequent discussions of the issues. Audette Lepage of the VIF deserves special thanks for her constant secretarial and organizing support, as does Susan Campbell for her assistance in providing research materials. We likewise thank Lynne Cohen for a very helpful round of copy editing of the penultimate draft. Members of the VIF Program Committee listened frequently to our progress reports and added helpful suggestions.

James Robertson of the U.K. was an early influence, and he also attended the Saskatchewan seminar. So was Tom Berger, through his work in the Canadian North, his involvement with the VIF and his attendance at the Saskatchewan seminar. Duncan Cameron read the entire manuscript and made many helpful suggestions. Many other people provided stimulus and support along the way, including Michael Asch, Doug Elias, Max Hedley,

Ray Jackson, Bill Nicholls, Grant Maxwell, Lyn Pinkerton, Steven Langdon, Liz Ross and Pamela White.

We owe an enormous debt to our friend, George McRobie, not only for freely sharing his immense knowledge and good sense with us but also for his constant support of our work in both good times and bad. Finally, the authors thank each other for the hours of interesting discussions on difficult points--always sustained by each other's good humor.

INTRODUCTION

No one doubts that the Western economies, and perhaps especially Canada's, have not been performing well lately. We seem to lurch from unemployment to inflation to energy crisis to high interest rates, and around again, like a pinball among the bumpers. Not surprisingly, we have turned increasingly to economists for word on the health of the economy, just as the family of the seriously ill seeks reassurance from the doctors. Like the hospital patient, the economy is carefully monitored. Every day the media tell us of its performance as indicated by the value of the dollar, of gold, of commodities and of stock market shares. We are informed of its performance every week by the bank rate, every month by the unemployment rate and the consumer price index, and every quarter by the balance of payments and trade and the gross national product (GNP). And every day another economist forecasts how these indicators might change in the next six months or a year and, by implication, how well off we can expect to be.

Unless we are among the few who stand to win or lose considerable sums each day on the basis of tiny fluctuations in exchange rates or stock prices, these indicators are not much of a guide to our well-being. Stock market rallies and the easing of interest rates have not resulted in a noticeable decline in unemployment. Having hooked our economy to high and rising energy prices, many now view steady prices and demand as bad for both business and public revenue. The goals of plenty, security, a clean environment, safe work--and better education leading to useful and interesting jobs--all seem more difficult to attain now, despite tremendous technological advances and economic growth which were supposed to bring about all of these things.

We are told, paradoxically, that as we become wealthier and

1

have more options from which to choose, we must become leaner and meaner. No institution and no person, it seems, can be spared the harsh necessity of becoming more productive and more competitive. Are these the new iron laws of economics?

Economics is often thought of, in everyday life, as a kind of calculus involving profits and losses, balance of payments, interest rates, wage rates, prices and so on. Above all, however, an economy is a set of relations among people. It is the customs, rules and institutions used by people to organize themselves to produce, distribute, exchange and consume things.

Older economies relied on such relations as family, kin and community to get things done. Of course, these arrangements produced many fewer and far simpler goods and services. What distinguishes a modern economy not only is the variety, complexity and sheer volume of its output but also its organization. We now rely heavily on very large and complex organizations to produce and distribute our output, and so our economic life has come to be dominated by giant corporations and governments. Family, kin and community play such a marginal role in our economic lives that many of us think of these institutions as social rather than economic. In effect, we think of "the economy" as being in the sphere of business and government.

Large corporations and governments have come to play an increasingly greater role in our lives in two ways. One way has been in their doing things that smaller institutions simply cannot do, especially with respect to complex industrial processes. We cannot expect to gather with a few friends and neighbors (no matter how clever and skilled) in the basement and set about producing jumbo jets or heavy turbines, nor drill down two miles for oil in the neighboring field. Nor could we expect to mass produce cars, toasters, pharmaceuticals or hockey skates in this manner. So in one sense, we might suppose that "the economy" --business--is a superstructure, built on the foundation of family and community activity, and doing the things that they cannot otherwise do.

A second way large organizations have affected our lives is in their now doing a great deal of what people have routinely done since the dawn of time, such as providing food, clothing, shelter and a wide range of personal and social services. This happened because it appeared that industrial mass production was cheaper and more efficient. It is now widely believed that families and communities have become obsolete as economic institutions because they are less efficient and productive than firms.

Therefore, they now play only a social role. In this view, the economic function of the family or household is limited to consuming the output of firms (corporations or enterprises) and providing labor for them by giving birth to, rearing and training children and by nurturing the adult worker. The success of the family as a social unit is now commonly judged by the quality of the labor it provides to the larger institutions, and by the quantity and conspicuousness of the goods and services it can buy back in exchange. (See Appendix A for an illustration of how the study of economics has treated the economic role of the household over time.)

The community, likewise, has only a social function left. Nowadays, when we think of community institutions, what comes to mind are the church, the school, the club or the sports association, not the office, the farm, the factory or the shop. So in this sense, "the economy" appears not as superstructure on an enduring foundation of family and community activity but as a replacement for them. In this view, industry and commerce drive out all other forms of economic endeavor because we are told the former are more efficient, and will continue to be so in the future. What is not industrialized now soon will be with technological and organizational advancements. Our basic concepts of modernization, development and progress rest on industrialization, with the result that family and community-based production of goods and services is almost automatically dismissed as antiquated and outmoded.

It is our belief that this view of formalization and industrialization as pervasive and inevitable not only is greatly exaggerated but would also be an undesirable outcome in the future because it undermines a vital part of our social fabric and leaves fundamental human needs unfulfilled.

The concept of industrialization as all-pervasive is inaccurate because it ignores a vast range of productive activity in our society that is not carried out by large corporations or governments and, indeed, is hardly recognized by them to exist. Such activity includes the domestic economy of the household and the local economy of the community. Taken together, most of the activities carried out in these areas may be thought of as comprising the "informal economy," in contrast to the formal, commercial and public sector economy. In the informal economy, goods and services are often exchanged without money transactions. When money is involved, it is to facilitate exchange, not to increase profits, so the drive to accumulate capital for its own sake is not present. Whereas the formal economy focuses solely on output, in the informal economy, how things are done, who receives the output and how people relate to one another are as important as what is produced. Informal production is highly decentralized, performed in small units and under community or household control. The informal economy is owner-operated, whether the owner is an individual, a household or a community. To central authorities, planners and economists, the informal economy, consisting as it does of many small autonomous units, is largely invisible and therefore unquantified and unrecorded.

Despite the ascendancy of mass markets and giant corporations, domestic and local economies still function. Indeed, informal economic activities often reappear when given the opportunity. The informal economy is not merely an appendage of the formal industrial economy; it operates according to quite different principles, although it is certainly affected by the formal economy. The simplistic distinctions developed in the formal economy between public and private, economic and social, production and consumption, and work and leisure do not work well outside of that economy. Worse, they hinder understanding of both how we actually live and how we might want to live. While the informal economy is no less essential to our well-being than the formal economy, it can easily be restricted, hobbled and distorted by the formal economy, unless the relationship between the two is rethought.

Most people idealize the sharing, comradeship, intimacy and mutual aid that are associated with family, community and friends. A good life is marked by an abundance of those contacts, occasions and relationships. Yet, the prevailing view in industrial society seems to be that the production of commodities is the prime means by which we can satisfy human needs, and since the formal economy is so good at producing commodities, it should be the focus of our public purpose. But satisfaction and purpose in life come not simply from consumption but from production and, in particular, from the social bonds and relations that are formed in the course of production. Consequently, if household and community are denied any significant role in production, and are relegated merely to consuming the output of the formal economy, then we will find less and less satisfaction in our family and community lives which no amount of increased consumption can remedy. If household and community are to be anything more than refuges from the rigors of formal economic life (or battlegrounds if the refuge function fails), then we have to rethink the place of households and community in economic life.

We believe that people seek satisfaction from economic activity not only in the amount of goods and services to which they can lay claim but also in the work processes and relationships they enter into by participating in economic activity. The free market is praised by many not only for its efficiency but also for its democratic nature: it provides goods and services in response to people's choices. Whether this is entirely true (and we do not believe it is) is not, however, of main concern here. For if one of the hallmarks of a democratic society is the ability to choose *what* goods and services we produce, surely another is the ability to choose *how* the goods and services are produced (and what kind of relationships we enter into in the course of economic activity).

There is, of course, the belief--and it is widespread in industrial societies--that work and production are necessarily unpleasant experiences for people, and that social well-being is measured simply by the standard of living (per capita income) which is the recompense for this unpleasantness. In effect, we trade away all of our rights, desires and satisfactions for eight hours a day in return for our wages with which we purchase our private pleasures in our leisure time.

Those who have rejected this vision of industrial society have proposed alternatives of essentially two types. One is to put a human face on industry; the other, to reduce the scale of enterprise.

Humanizing industry has been one of the goals of the trade union movement to the extent that it has fought for safety and dignity on the job and greater control over production itself. Sometimes, however, trade unions have sacrificed this goal in favor of higher pay and benefits. In other words, they have valued their members' satisfaction by means of commodities more highly than their satisfaction by means of control over their work relationships. Of course, they have been strongly encouraged to follow this course by employers and governments, who have always sought to reserve to themselves the rights of management. However, there are some philosophies of management (more common in Europe and Japan than in North America) which have promoted worker satisfaction and involvement in the job as a means of improving productivity.

Determining to what extent people can truly exercise control and choice in their formal economic relations is beyond the scope of this book. Instead, we want to show that the informal economy by its very nature provides alternative economic structures and relationships to those in the formal economy, and that is why many people prefer the informal economy.

There are, however, many obstacles confronting people who wish to exercise their preference for dividing time between formal and informal activity. In part, these are structural and institutional--the customs, regulations and policies that have arisen with respect to the organization of work, the distribution of social welfare benefits and sexual discrimination at home and at work.

They include, as well, the ways we identify and measure what is "economic," the current relationship between work, employment and income, and the system of taxation and public finance. The spectacular growth of an international system of production, marketing and trade, in a widening array of goods and services, is a particularly important force working against the maintenance and development of less formal systems of production and distribution.

The problem also occurs at the individual and household level. Since all of us participate in both the formal and informal economies to varying degrees, what governs the mix in each case? How do we choose, juggle or get pushed or locked into any particular mix? Is the mix we have the one we want or the one we must put up with? How can we broaden the choices in this important area of our lives?

To answer these questions we have to reexamine some of the basic goals of economic life. The economic news and commentary we hear every day emphasize the goals of more jobs, profits, income and trade. But these are means, not ends. They are the means by which people obtain what they want--from the basics like food, shelter and health care to entertainment, cultural and intellectual stimuli, sensual and aesthetic pleasure, and social status. The informal economy can and does provide some of these things.

CHAPTER ONE

PREVAILING CONSERVATIVE NOSTRUMS

A broad spectrum of programs and solutions from right to left are being urged upon us by economists to solve our economic problems. But many are inclined to disbelieve the claims of economists and politicians about who is to blame or what is the solution. Perhaps one of the reasons is that many no longer believe that the problems or the solutions are "economic" as the term is conventionally used. For example, the Canadian Conference of Catholic Bishops has attracted national attention by talking about the ethical issues of economics to which many economists have responded irritably by asking what do bishops know about economics.

While large corporations, trade associations and producer organizations continue to use the political structure to further their economic goals, ordinary citizens in the political process-- local or national--seem to be preoccupied not with economic problems but with what are generally called social issues: education, pensions, health care, housing, human rights, nuclear weapons, delinquency, marriage breakdown, pornography, the environment and so forth. We suggest that people are less and less responsive to the existing array of economic "solutions" because they no longer believe these solutions will work. And even if they did work they probably would not solve the fundamental problems people are identifying in society. Indeed, they might even make them worse. It is as though economic and social issues and their analyses are ships passing in the night.

Ironically, the most popular remedies for curing the economy are those that would widen even further the split between economic and social concerns. The trend in industrialized

7

countries is to elect conservative governments promising to get the economy back on the tracks by making preeminent once again the decision-making powers of free markets. This increases the role of the formal economy and diminishes or ignores support to the informal.

The driving force and appeal of conservative governments is found in their promises to reestablish the past and bring back the romantic "good old days," primarily the result of small-town informal ways. But a greater reliance on free markets today will lead us farther away, not closer to informal and more sociable ways of doing business.

It is easy to understand the appeal of conservative governments--to go back to simpler times--as a backlash to decades of liberal administrations promising that big government would collectively solve all the nation's economic and social problems. And progress was made on many problems, but in doing so the methods and structures used created different problems in their wake.

The political way out is now to combine the best of the conservative appeal with what was worthy of big liberal governments. What the conservative trend brings that is good is the emphasis once again on main street--on small business and local initiatives, on the importance of the individual, the household and community groups. What is wrong is the total faith placed in the so-called free forces of the market to bring about this desired change in emphasis. Under free markets, much main street activity, while providing a more informed social context, also provided low wages, autocratic employers and discriminatory hiring and pay practices.

What was good about liberal governments was their emphasis on collective, not market, decision-making processes. What was bad was that collective processes and the institutions required to facilitate them grew too big, too formal and too insensitive so that people felt collective decision making was no longer sufficiently democratic. Household and community started to wither in importance as the bureaucratic structures and practices of big government began to resemble those of big business.

The assumption behind the solution contained in this book is that we can best solve our economic and social problems by heeding the best of conservative and liberal beliefs. And this can only be accomplished through smaller structures and collective processes that are closer to the community which yield more informal, appropriate and democratic solutions.

The Conservative Political and Economic Trend

Three competing streams of thought dominate conservative economic agendas: supply-side, monetarist and post-Keynesian fiscal restraint. Of the three streams, *supply-side* is the least generous in terms of directly considering the human or social consequences of economic decisions. Social conditions in this schema are best attended to indirectly by maintaining strong free markets. Private charity and limited public programs centered around social "problems" can deal with any residual social needs. Supply-siders want to return to a laissez-faire world which they claim will provide incentives for people to amass great wealth. Like President Reagan in the U.S. and the Fraser Institute in Canada, they believe fervently in the necessity of financial incentives. These come in two forms--carrots for the rich and sticks for the poor.

Extreme supply-siders would remove virtually all assistance and support for the poor, honestly believing they are doing them a favor.[1] The poor are expected, in turn, to industriously react to the lifting of these pesky disincentives and in gratitude go on to accumulate great wealth. Supply-side economic strategies propose to bring about the end of inflation and unemployment by providing so much private incentive for rich and poor alike that the economy will prosper and the resulting cornucopia will restrain price increases and produce full employment.

Supply-side economics masks its ideology with dubious assumptions concerning human behavior. It flatly states that economic growth and personal achievement can be fostered only when individuals are encouraged to keep all they produce or the monetary equivalent of it. Supply-side economic theory is based on this fragile assumption: no financial incentives, no economy. However, the true assumption behind supply-side ideology is most likely this: "Wealthy people enjoy their wealth, and they never tire of wanting more." If supply-side policies clearly stated this assumption, the theory might consequently be more believable.

Moving from right to center among the three fashionable conservative streams, *monetarism* in general is not as fervently laissez-faire as supply-side economics. But defenders of monetarism, such as the American economist Milton Friedman, differ little ideologically from supply-siders except in their approaches to curbing inflation. In Canada, monetarism is associated primarily with the central bank, the Bank of Canada.

Theoretically, monetarism could contain a direct concern for the social and human side of economics. But generally, like supply-side thought, it believes in the "trickle-down" theory of benefits resulting from the interplay of commercial free market forces and economic growth. Technically, monetarism espouses only that the course of the economy--price stability, growth, full employment--can be guided almost exclusively by altering the size of a nation's money supply. But, in fact, it is difficult to find within the monetarist doctrine anything but a firm belief in the sanctity of the marketplace. Here, a very small role is assigned to the public sector, collective decision making and the quality of human relationships, since the major objective is increasing real output within a commercial framework.

In general, monetarism proposes that lightly controlled market forces can best solve our economic and social problems. The Governor of the Bank of Canada in public speeches has requested government cooperation through spending restraint, and less interference with market forces by such things as marketing boards and minimum wages.

However, for those who believe that it was something other than market forces that led to the small improvements in the lives of women and minority groups in this century, it is difficult to become a card-carrying monetarist. It is small comfort to the poor and the disabled to go to sleep each night believing that market forces are silently at work protecting their standards of living and liberties.

The third prevailing stream of conservative thought is represented by post-Keynesian *fiscal restraint.* Most legitimate restrainers--excluding monetarists who perpetually seek government restraint--are in the Keynesian⁻ intellectual tradition. Keynesians accept the need for government intervention in order to keep the economy on a stable growth course and, in fact, most post-World War II economic policy until the late 1970s has been unabashedly of the Keynesian variety.

Keynesians believe that when the economy is sluggish and unemployment is high, governments must incur budget deficits. On the other hand, when economies are overheated and prices are rising, it is considered proper to run budget surpluses to cool the total demands on productive capacity. Keynesians are not too upset if, within the overall level of government expenditures, some are earmarked for social purposes. But a Keynesian is still a strong believer in market forces and commercial profit, and government expenditures should never become so large as to interfere with the normal working of these forces.

Most policy makers within the restraint school today are, in fact, post-Keynesians. Post-Keynesian policy believes that government has a role to play in stabilizing the economy through budget surpluses or deficits; but it also believes that governments must regularly intervene in the economy to assure at least a minimum provision of social goods and services as well as a fairer distribution of income.[2]

Unfortunately, or perhaps inevitably, much post-Keynesian policy has become restraint policy. Some of this change in outlook has reluctantly come about as a result of political pressure or panic, but some of it is through an attraction with monetarism and supply-side economics. This veer to the right is probably attributable to the fact that the post-Keynesian world has fallen apart. Keynesian economics does not easily reconcile unemployment and inflation; in fact, they are considered opposites. You can have one or the other, but not both simultaneously. Keynes himself would have felt intellectually uncomfortable with today's "stagflation" in which economic growth is often accompanied by net job reduction.

J.K. Galbraith, a leading American economist and author, some time ago laid bare one of the roots of today's unemployment/inflation problems.[3] He revealed that we no longer have the competitive market forces which in the past supposedly produced falling wages and prices when the economy was sluggish and unemployment existed. Instead, we have large corporations and unions capable of holding up prices and wages even as unemployment rises to historic levels.

At least until the election of the current conservative government, post-Keynesian policy in Canada had dealt with the unemployment/inflation dilemma primarily by engaging in expansionary fiscal policies--large deficits--but had curiously allowed the Bank of Canada to pursue contradictory tight money policies especially between 1975 and 1983. As a consequence, the two policy approaches worked against each other, resulting at the worst point in a 13 percent inflation rate and almost a million and a half unemployed.

Having had limited success in playing its expansionary policies against the Bank's dominant tight money stance, post-Keynesian policy was led to abandon its convictions and embrace, with varied enthusiasm, the policies of the new right. Public support of the new right economics (which has always been much stronger in the U.S. than Canada), combined with the government's lack of success in controlling the economy, have intimidated post-Keynesian policy. Unwilling to raise taxes in order to cover the large deficits, and increasingly being lectured by the monetarists for adopting contrary policies, governments have been faced with the choice of either asking the Bank of Canada to ease up on its monetary restraint or supporting, through fiscal restraint, the Bank's policy of cooling the economy. Governments now tend to follow the Bank's lead.

Nonetheless, in comparing the likely and intended policy outcomes of these three conservative economic schools, those of the post-Keynesian restrainers--at least in human and social terms--are the least damaging. The current restraint policy stance flows less from ideological commitment than from con-fusion. We should perhaps call it reluctant restraint; the orderly Keynesian world has fallen apart and strategies are being devised hastily without a new coherent framework.

The three schools of thought espouse somewhat different policy measures, but their policy impact on human relationships and informal economic activity is similar on two accounts. First, in the North American mixed economy, where private decision making directly accounts for probably about two-thirds of all "economic" decisions, the rightward shift of current economic policy will result in a strengthening of this type of decision making. The marketplace, guided by commercial profits, will make more decisions. And this process is highly compatible with less government (collective) decision making and reduced public sector activity. Secondly, there is often a stated hope that family and voluntary activity at the community level (in other words, the informal economy) will increase and offset the reduced collective provision of services. However, this fervent hope is seldom followed up with suggestions as to how the informal economy will obtain the resources necessary to carry the increased load.

To understand how the formal economy makes decisions, it is necessary to understand the full meaning of the phrases, commercial or private profit. A profit is generated by a firm when the private revenue from production exceeds the private cost. If producers are allowed--as they are in Western countries --to retain their profits as they please, then the environment and stimulus exists for private economic decision making based on commercial profitability. The resurgence of conservative eco-nomic doctrines says we should have more decision making of the commercial type, and less of the collective type.

Increased private decision making will not likely lead to a

more informal, appropriate and democratic society. What gets produced in the private economy is what is appropriate to profitability, not community need. We will succeed in achieving an abundance of low-cost fun flights to the sun, but not low-cost day care for ordinary families, nor the unfettered application of technology to assist people with disabilities.

The new conservative economics counters that people get what they demand. After all, the marketplace is the truest democracy in the world, where people vote daily for goods and services with their dollar bills. But it conveniently ignores the fact that this democracy is founded on a process which discourages equal voting rights. The upper 20 percent of most industrialized countries' populations control over 40 percent of the financial ballots (income), while the bottom 20 percent control less than 5 percent.[4] This is hardly the basis for a sound democracy.

A strengthening of the decision-making process guided by commercial profitability will further concentrate the control over goods and service production in the hands of upper-income citizens. Lower-income citizens by necessity rely heavily on the collective provision of goods and services, and as this sector shrinks in importance they suffer. The results of the conservative policies followed in the U.S. and U.K. are now bearing this out.

These new conservative policies will not only affect the nature of what is produced. All decisions concerning the ratio of labor and capital employed, the type and level of technology used, the wages and types of employment for women and the disabled, whether production is centrally or locally based and controlled, as well as the physical conditions of work, are guided by what is most appropriate to commercial profit. Market decision making does not directly take into consideration the quality of life of workers and their families. It will simply be a coincidence if the work force as a whole is better off under a system of strengthened private decision making.

A return to more decision making based on commercial profit would reinforce the biggest failure of privately organized work processes: the neglect of household and community differences, needs and aspirations. Free-market economic theory lumps labor together with capital and land as if it were a homogeneous and inanimate factor of production. This practice undoubtedly stems from the belief that work itself is of little value; only the output from work and the wage it confers have value. Output and profits are the glamorous ends of the industrial process; work is only a grubby means.

Another area of decision making that conservative policies will entrust to the formal forces of the market is the distribution of goods and services. In a free market economy, goods and services are distributed according to income. Large incomes command large shares of society's goods and services; small incomes command otherwise. With the exception of a relatively small and grudging amount of income directed through government transfers, income is acquired through employment or the ownership of wealth.

A greater reliance on the formal economy to distribute income can only widen the already unequal distribution of income and wealth in Canada and other industrialized nations. Conservatives frequently acknowledge that some people are rather badly treated by the market system, but extremists consider this an incentive for the badly treated to do something positive about their predicament.

Conservative economic philosophy, while staunchly forbidding any direct intervention in the formal economy's income distribution mechanism, talks about granting assistance to the poor through public income maintenance schemes. Milton Friedman favors a comprehensive negative income tax scheme which he proposes will replace all existing income security programs.[5]

But even residual income security schemes such as this, which do not directly interfere with market forces as minimum wages do, are not actively endorsed by conservative policies. Conservative thought does not strongly advocate a more equal distribution of income. And the reason is to be found in a simple "catch-22" scenario.

The state is forbidden to interfere directly with market forces because this creates economic distortions and curbs entrepreneurial liberties. Income redistribution, if it occurs, must take place after the fact and indirectly through tax/transfer policies. But redistribution means levying taxes and distributing the proceeds to the poor. And since taxes curb the work incentives of the rich and income transfers stultify the incentives of the poor, this redistribution process also leads to economic distortions. Alas, we can do nothing! However, at least there is now a presumed economic rationale for not redistributing income; the decision is not seen to be simply based on greed or mean-spiritedness, but rather on sound economic growth theory.

Control of the economy through most conservative policies also means lower taxes and deregulation of industry. While enterpreneurs may make more money as a result, fewer regulations also lead to more pollution and environmental degradation, increased occupational health hazards, more freedom to discriminate and abuse human rights and less income and employment security.

Conservatives, by encouraging private sector forces, propose to expand their way out of all and any inflation/unemployment dilemma, but this raises three questions. First, there is no evidence that indiscriminate economic growth pursued through the private sector is non-inflationary. Secondly, some economic studies, such as those by the international, intergovernmental body, the Organization for Economic Cooperation and Development (OECD), suggest that much of today's new investment will be job-reducing, so that while GNP may increase, employment may not.[6] Consequently, market incentives may generate more unemployment and increase income inequalities. Thirdly, we must question the desire and need for more "economic growth" as measured by GNP. More satisfying and productive lives can be achieved through more informal economic activities and an increase in "outputs" not quantifiable or normally thought of as consumption goods.

What kind of society will conservative policies ultimately create for us? Although they present a somewhat exaggerated picture, the novels of Charles Dickens and Victor Hugo--and within living memory of many, the Great Depression--provide examples of such societies. These examples demonstrate the sad conditions of societies based solely on the pursuit of commercial profits.

In particular among the conservative streams of economic policy, monetarist and fiscal restraint policies have been applied to temporarily contract the economy--that is, kill it off and cool it out until financial incentives can take hold and boom the formal economy. But they propose to contract it rather indiscriminately by using big levers and letting the chips fall where they may, which means on the most vulnerable.

The stated purpose of contraction (the consequences of which Canada suffered particularly during the period 1980-83) is to reduce inflation through increasing unemployment and interest rates. The rationale behind raising interest rates and creating unemployment is to reduce the demands on labor and capital markets. As slack occurs in these markets--that is, as unemployment rises, as investment is choked off, as small businesses fail, as the rates of mortgage foreclosures become widespread--

market forces act to moderate wages and prices. A "learning experience" takes place. And workers and businesspeople, not wanting to obtain this experience first hand through joining the growing army of the unemployed or the bankrupt and the dispossessed, reduce their expectations, behave more moderately and increase their productivity and efficiency. At least that is the theory behind conservative economic policy.

There are, however, two serious problems that have resulted from the application of this harsh policy. The first lies in the procedure for choosing those who are to get the "learning experience" the hard way--that is, the selection of the unemployed, the bankrupt, the dispossessed. Certainly, people have not all been evenly affected by recent recessions. Households and businesses with large incomes and small debts insulate themselves from a contraction more effectively than can the poor, the young, the disabled, the small and the unskilled. These people are forced to fall back on what remains of their informal economic networks which over the years have been eroded by policies designed to favor formal economic activity. However, in some areas it is encouraging to witness a resurgence of informal economic activity stimulated by the failures in the formal economy.

The second shortcoming with conservative restraint policy is this: after having succeeded in raising unemployment beyond 13 percent, lowering inflation below 6 percent and achieving close to zero growth, then what? Do we stay in this depressed state forever? Obviously not, because politicians cannot allow this situation to persist for long--although the U.K. seems to be going for a record. As growth continues to stall and unemployment remains high, we will be forced to slowly expand the economy, adopting favorite conservative financial incentives along the way to encourage private investment. But it seems inevitable that inflation will eventually creep back and force a cessation of expansion. And we will be back to high unemployment and a precariously stalled economy. If prices and wages are not really determined by market forces but are instead administered by large corporations, unions and associations of self-interests, there is no reason to expect that prices and wages will not rise again during expansion.

The major flaw in conservative "stop-go" economic management is the fact that the wrong people are sent to "school" during the contractionary phase. The people who set wages and prices in the formal economy do not suffer all that badly, and the prospect of another round of contraction does not seriously moderate their behavior, at least not for long. During downturns, no permanent and significant structural changes are made in the way we divide the pie into profits, rents, wages, fees, interest payments, perquisites, taxes and so on. Consequently, the uncontrolled fight for larger income shares is renewed once the formal economy expands.

An economy controlled by successively induced contractions and expansions produces a boom and bust society. This type of economic behavior is not the mark of a compassionate and intelligent society. We end up with temporarily reduced prices, a balanced budget and a stable dollar, but also with a high level of unemployment, reduced health care, an inadequate housing stock, fewer affordable educational opportunities, inferior day-care facilities and increased marital distress. But by conservative economic doctrines these must be regarded as successful policy outcomes!

Ironically, many of the economic policies promoted by the mainstream left also serve to keep the basic framework of the formal economy intact. They accept a mixed economy and would simply intervene more strenuously and try to put a human face on capitalism. Social democrats' chief difference with conservative post-Keynesian restrainers is that they identify many more areas for intervention in a mixed economy and are concerned more about unemployment than inflation. Job creation is a high priority and, where free enterprise does not create jobs, governments should do this through a combination of incentives, regulations and direct investments through Crown corporations. Social democrats, in contrast to conservatives, are inclined to believe that poverty and unemployment are not the result of individual failure but of social conditions such as the unequal distribution of income, wealth and opportunity. Consequently, they believe more strongly than post-Keynesians in social programs financed by corporate and progressive income taxes.

In practice, social democracy in both Canada and Western Europe has disappointed many of its supporters and converted few of its opponents. This is chiefly because, in its determination to control private enterprise, it has relied heavily on the instruments of the state. Nowadays, social democracy (or what its opponents choose to call "socialism") is firmly identified in the public mind with big government, big unions, and centralized, formal and unresponsive bureaucracies.

When it comes to public relations, corporate strategy, conditions of employment and service to the public, there is little to distinguish Crown corporations like Air Canada and Canadian National Railways from their counterparts in private industry. Nor to the average person is there any apparent difference between publicly owned provincial monopolies like Ontario Hydro and Alberta Government Telephones and regulated privately owned monopolies like Bell Canada. Experience with nationalized industries in modern Western economies seems to prove that they are neither more efficient, nor do they serve substantially different social ends than private corporations. Consequently, nationalization no longer appeals to many as a solution to either economic or social problems.

Financing public programs from corporate profits seems fine when corporations are making (or at least declaring) profits. But when they are not, the difference between social democratic governments and post-Keynesian restrainers seems to disappear. As well, the very process of redistribution under social democracy is fraught with perceived inequities. There is no end of complaining and griping about allegedly hard-earned money being taken away to support worthless programs, lazy and incompetent bureaucrats, and shiftless idlers on welfare. The more insistent the redistribution, the louder become the complaints. We seem to have to choose, in this zero-sum world, between the cries of the haves who claim they are being deprived and those of the have-nots who claim they are not getting enough.[7]

Apart from the cost of social programs and who is called upon to pay for them, however, is the issue of their size, inflexibility and unresponsiveness. Roles traditionally played by the family and the community are taken over by state institutions, often beneficially but sometimes not. And those who are supposed to benefit from the welfare state are sometimes afraid to deal with it because it is bureaucratic and interventionist. To many people, the cost of the safety net is high in terms of bureaucratic snooping and interference.

One hears less these days from the more radical left--those who do not believe it possible to give capitalism a human face and who propose to replace it with some form of socialism. But if classical Marxist theory and the socialist systems of the Eastern bloc countries are anything to go by, the informal economy is not simply ignored, it is opposed. Curiously, one reason for this opposition, and possibly the most important one, is precisely that offered by capitalist societies, although for different reasons: the family and the local community are inefficient producers. Classical socialists believed that a society capable of producing superabundance would remove all need for toil and all tendencies towards exploitation and inequality. Consequently, such figures as Engels and Lenin emphasized the need to "unleash the forces of production" so as to create abundance. Capitalism was condemned not only because of its inequalities--but also because with its cycles of expansion and recession, its unemployment and its foundation on the nuclear family (which kept women in the home and out of the labor force), it was seen to be inefficient. The key to abundance was industrial organization. Amazingly, Lenin was a great admirer of Frederick Taylor, the apostle of American business management and of time and motion studies. Some early British socialists, especially the Fabians, also admired Taylor's approach. In the early years of the Soviet revolution, radical attempts were made to alter the position of women in society, and many socialists of that time advocated communal living because domestic labor could thus be industrialized.

But can it be that both right and left, capitalists and socialists--and everyone from the American futurist Herman Kahn to Engels and Lenin--agree that the only way forward lies with ever greater industrialization? Today, we are exhorted to get aboard the high technology revolution, get on with energy megaprojects on the frontier and become superorganized and specialized so as to be competitive in the international economy. We are told these are the keys to jobs and prosperity and that we are in grave danger of being left behind in the race. Those who question are dismissed as Luddites, smashers of machinery and hence of society. Whether we live in Poland, Chile or Canada, we are told we should work harder and longer for less. The inducements are different, but not the message.

The common theme of the industrial nirvana is the emphasis on production in the context of a mass society. Whether it is the new right's devotion to the free market or the old left's devotion to industrial organization, we are encouraged to devote our productive effort more and more to the mass economy and less and less to our domestic and community life. For both the free market and industrial organization are the institutional mechanisms by which strangers are thrown together and induced to work with or for one another. Because this method is deemed the most efficient for production we are paid a wage or fee in reward for spending our time in this way and can then purchase what is needed. Consequently, we are discouraged from taking care of our own needs in a more informal context.

Yet, there are many critiques of the formal economy from

all points on the spectrum. They come from conservative philosophers like George Grant, from both liberals and social democrats (who are rethinking traditional policies and approaches) and from what is loosely called the new left--as well as from anarchists.[8] They are also coming from a number of churches (for example, the Canadian Catholic bishops' statement on the economy).[9]

CHAPTER TWO

THE NATURE OF FORMAL ECONOMIC ACTIVITY

Chapter One has drawn a relationship between political philosophies and economic policies. We categorized the two main approaches to the economy as formal and informal without defining these terms very closely. In this chapter, we begin to make a clearer distinction between formal and informal activity by looking at some of the key features of formal activity that affect the structuring of our daily lives. Examined will be such factors as the isolation of production and consumption roles, the extensive use of contracts, the effects of a competitive environment, the results of specialized economic roles (and the deskilling that results), the use of hierarchical and authoritative organizational structures, and the constant pursuit of modernization and growth.

Producers and Consumers

The goods and services which are commonly exchanged in the formal economy are, for the most part, produced by complex industrial processes. These specialized processes require the labor of many different people, with different capabilities, whose work must be coordinated and integrated in factories, bureaucratic offices and shops. The formal economy is dominated by large units in the form of big business corporations or government agencies, which are organized and directed from the top down.

One consequence of this type of economic organization is

that most people, instead of selling things they make themselves or services they provide directly, sell their capacity to work as if it were a commodity for which they are paid wages or salaries. So the formal economy is for the most part a wage economy. And a very large part of this wage income is never even concerned with production and distribution, but rather with finance, marketing and exchange.

Economists have developed a simple model of how this works. There are two sets of actors--producers and consumers. They are organized respectively as firms and households. Firms (whether large or small corporations or owner-operated businesses) act to maximize their profits, along with growth and accumulation. This is achieved by constantly increasing productivity and efficiency within the firm and by gaining more effective control over whatever might affect the firm. Households are said to want to maximize their satisfaction--to obtain the most pleasure from spending the money they have at their disposal. Households are never viewed as producers, only firms are. (See Appendix A.) The essential piece of information required to get these units interacting with one another is price. If there is perfect knowledge of prices, everyone can begin to engage in what the father of modern economics, Adam Smith, claimed is their inherent propensity "to truck or barter," in order to get on with the business of maximizing profits and satisfaction.

In the ideal economic world, there are countless producers and consumers, each motivated by individual self-interest and in competition with one another. The market--the arena of all this activity--is assumed to be totally impersonal. In principle, our willingness to purchase something should be unaffected by whether it is made by neighbors or strangers or by people we like or dislike. Purchases should only depend on the price and quality of the commodity itself. Hired labor's personal attributes, other than those related to the performance of the job itself, should not be considered important. Merit alone should decide. To choose friends or relatives over strangers is nepotism--an interference with the market. If we sell property, we should sell only to the highest bidder without favoritism to family, friends and neighbors.

For these impersonal transactions to take place voluntarily and knowingly rather than by coercion, four conditions must be met. First, information about the prices and attributes of commodities must be equally available to all. Secondly, there must be numerous and autonomous buyers and sellers, none of whom can be big enough to affect price and quantity in the marketplace. Thirdly, there must be security of property. Fourthly, there must be an enforceable system of contracts to ensure that people live up to their commercial undertakings.

Contracts

An obvious feature of the formal economy, and specifically of modern life in Western industrialized nations, is that it brings together, in a frequent and sustained way, people who otherwise do not and cannot know one another on the basis of kinship, neighborhood or friendship. The relations of producer and consumer, buyer and seller, employer and employee are, for the most part, anonymous and impersonal. Yet, like all other human relationships they require trust, confidence and predictability in order to work. Because the formal economy is impersonal, however, we cannot expect those qualifications to be based on intimate knowledge, shared experience, kinship obligations or personal loyalty. Nor can behavior or motivation be accurately predicted on the basis of a person's social status. So there must be a system of contracts which will ensure that these rela-tionships will work. There must also be a way of enforcing these contracts, for in relationships with strangers a handshake is not an adequate guarantee.

Contracts are a part of everyday life in the formal economy, and a substantial amount of working time is spent in formulating, negotiating, implementing and enforcing them. Every time we buy a subway token, a sheet of plywood or a meal in a restaurant, we enter into a set of contractual relationships with a lot of other people and organizations. Since we do not expect complications to arise from these oridinary daily trans-actions, we seldom bother to acknowledge these contracts explicitly with each transaction. In some cases, the contract is specified in summary form, but we do not bother to examine it. How many of us read the "fine print" on a warranty, an airline ticket, a credit card or an insurance policy? When these transactions do not work out as expected, however, we start reading the fine print or hire a lawyer to do it for us. Very often in these cases, we are surprised and upset by what we learn about contracts. We are dismayed not only because the deck appears stacked in favor of the large organization and against the private individual, but also because the contract permits no exception and takes no account of our particular circumstances.

Many transactions in the formal economy, however, involve very explicit, detailed contracts. For example, a typical collective agreement between labor and management includes not just a schedule of pay and benefits. It also contains a detailed set of rules which specify who has the authority over whom and to do what, under what conditions certain tasks shall be performed, by whom and with what facilities and what recourse the parties have in the event of disagreement.

Business and corporate transactions are almost never based on just a handshake. A contract to produce something, exchange something or provide services is a document that normally requires extensive negotiation and financial and legal expertise. An agreement to build fighter aircraft or a hydro-electric generating station, or to sell wheat to the Soviet Union or plastic containers to a soap manufacturer, can take months or years of preparation and be hundreds of pages thick.

As commercial transactions so often involve great numbers of people from different places and backgrounds, the contracts which govern them cannot be idiosyncratic or vernacular, as a verbal agreement between friends might be. Great care and attention must, therefore, be paid to the wording of the terms and specifications so as to minimize the possibility of misinterpretation. Standards of measurement and conventions of terminology and phrasing have arisen on the basis of decades, even centuries of precedents. The more one learns of these common (and indeed increasingly uniform) conventions and language, the better one is able to function in the formal economy.

These institutional requirements of the formal economy promote certain relationships and behavior among people. First, as we have already pointed out, formal economic institutions are based on the anonymity of people. They are institutions designed to enable perfect strangers to operate on a common basis with respect to production, distribution and exchange. Commercial relations are anonymous relations--"cash and carry." Price is the only information the system needs in order to work. Love, joy, devotion, compassion and spirituality are irrelevant "information" in a system based on commercial market principles. There is no mutual obligation beyond price and contract. There is no community, only individuals, each in competition with all others. Mutual obligations and aid, like community itself, are relegated to the personal sphere--they have nothing to do with "the economy."

This is not to say that friendship, honor or compassion are absent from the formal economy--only that they exist for reasons apart from, and perhaps in spite of, the needs or logic of "the economy."

Competition

It is assumed that within the formal economy competition is the essence of commercial market activity. As consumers, individuals must compete with one another for the most things and the best bargains. As producers, firms must compete with one another to sell more things, get a bigger market share, make more profits and grow bigger. As nations, we must compete with one another in the technology race, the productivity race, the growth race, the space race and the arms race. People and groups who do not care to join these races, thinking them unimportant or dangerous, may even be decried as poor team players--or worse, drags on the economy.

This is the zero-sum economy, where for every winner there must be a loser. We do, of course, impose some limits on competitive behavior in some spheres of the economy, but we are unwilling or unable to do so in others. So it is common to refer to competition in the formal economy as "cut-throat" and be proud of it. And there is a cult of machismo celebration of the ability to survive in this world.

Specialization and Deskilling

The logic of the formal economy promotes growth through specialization. The major economic blocs have moved rapidly towards an international division of labor with highly centralized, specialized production and long-distance trade. These shifts account for a growing share of total economic activity. The large organizations in our society--whether public or private--thus keep getting larger and more remote. What used to be made locally is now made in Taiwan or Brazil. The local, owner-operated hardware store is now a franchised outlet of a major chain with its head office in another province or state. The locus of responsibility for things also becomes diffuse. A seemingly simple item like a child's book is written in the U.K., illustrated in West Germany, printed in Japan, published in the U.S. and identified by a universal cataloguing system and product code. While that book may be merely an interesting illustration of the international division of labor, such diversified responsibility for the production and transport of hazardous products, for example, seems rather less benevolent.

The division of labor in the factory and office, as well as regionally and internationally, has led to a high degree of specialization in work. Rare is the job description which calls for the Renaissance Man. What is usually wanted are people who are either highly skilled at a particular task or who are prepared to accept repetitive routine work at a single task for long periods of time. The higher the level of the job, the more likely it is that substantial experience and specialized education and training are required. Even though it seems that more and more people are changing their careers at some point, through necessity or choice, at any one time in their lives they are paid to do only one thing. All their other skills, interests and attributes are of little interest to the labor market. This specialization is closely related to the rigidity of work roles. Employers and trade unions share an interest in maintaining strict boundaries about who shall do what. This is especially true where unions are organized along craft lines, or by job categories such as in the public service.

While certain jobs, especially the more prestigious and rewarding ones, require a greater diversity of skills and talents, this diversity is still limited to what is required on the job and for the firm. Indeed, these jobs may be so demanding that many of those who hold them have little interest and few responsibilities in life apart from their work. Their social relations may be limited to their work associates, excluding family, community and friends. This too is a form of specialization that occurs in the formal economy.

The consequence of these tendencies towards specialization is too often the deskilling of people in many other aspects of their lives. We have come to depend heavily on the wage packet for the most elementary of life's needs. Without jobs, and the pay checks that come with them, many would be unable to feed, shelter and clothe themselves. Money becomes a substitute for competence in everyday living. Jobs are specialized and compartmentalized so that only a few actually produce a complete good or service at work; most are producing only a part or component of an end product.

Where we do not or cannot produce the things we need, we come to depend on large and remote organizations over which, as individuals, we have relatively little control and about which we have little understanding. In effect, we delegate control and authority to others who provide us with life's basic needs, material and otherwise. Some of us, skilled or unskilled at work, require many things away from work to be prepackaged--the essentials of life, entertainment, diversion--because we are unable to meet these needs on our own time or through our own initiative.

Such a state of specialization, many would argue, is the price of prosperity and choice, and they may be right. After all, many of us choose to pay this price, and some of us do not fully realize we are paying any price at all. The formal economy offers challenges, new opportunities and excitement. It rewards the successful with prestige, power, material wealth, freedom and choice. For some, the formal economy is the only option seen to be available. Even a dull boring job gets one out of the house and brings a pay check in at the end of the week.

Authority and Hierarchy

The prevailing view of industrial organization in Canada is that in order for the economy to work, there must be an hierarchical system of power, authority and responsibility, adherence to rules and procedures and a system of discipline imposed from the top down. Only in the small new organizations do we see innovative approaches to the organization of work and a freer and more casual atmosphere with respect to matters such as work roles and intiatives, lines of authority or mode of dress. The larger and more established the organization, the more bureaucratic and inflexible is it likely to be. There will be less room, especially at the lower levels, for initiative, creativity and self-expression. There are, of course, exceptions at both ends of the scale. Every organization has its own style of management, but these exceptions tend to prove the rule.

This hierarchical authoritarian system has been a response to a situation in which people are thrown together as strangers.

Labor is highly mobile. People are brought together from many neighborhoods, and even many parts of the country, into a single work force. They may not stay in one job for long. They are promoted or transferred within the organization, or leave to join another. So hierarchy and discipline are a means of getting people to deal with one another in their work roles, rather than as individuals. Specified behavior is required towards someone because he or she is the incumbent in a particular job, rather than because of his or her personal qualities.

Modernization and Growth

Whatever we like or do not like about the formal economy, the economists' way of thinking about it has so dominated popular thought that we have come to accept a surprisingly one-dimensional view of society. In this conventional view, national economies are made up simply of firms and households. Firms produce goods and services, and households consume them. The household (or the family, the presumed social organization of the household) is also expected to reproduce labor, that is, give birth to children and rear them, and to nourish and nurture the adult worker.

Because conventional economics assumes producers and consumers to be mutually exclusive categories, and each household or firm to act solely to maximize its own welfare, it tends to dismiss evidence of cooperation, mutual aid and solidarity. The sense of community and tradition, and the economic organization and function of family and kinship beyond the limits of the household, are treated as irrelevant or even illusory. There is an assumption that all economic relationships are commercial relationships. (See Appendix A.) Conversely, non-commercial relationships, which have nothing to do with economics, are considered purely social. Thus, the classic "economic man" is really a tautology which results from defining economic activity as only that which occurs in the marketplace for commercial purposes, and then from observing only the behavior that occurs there.

We can now begin to see why our lives, in the conventional view, are rigidly divided between the economic and the social, and between work and leisure. In an industrially organized society, work is production, leisure is consumption. Work is even considered a disutility--something unpleasant that we must be induced to perform. Commercial profit is the means by which we are so induced. We seek compensation--a wage, salary or fee--for giving our capacity to work over to someone else's direction for a specified period of time. With this compensation we can purchase the means of subsistence. We have given up some of our time and allowed some of the skills to lapse, which we would normally devote to subsistence, in order to go to work. Further, we are compensated in order to consume things, and, hence, enjoy our time off from work. Few can imagine pleasure deriving from work or things of value being produced during leisure.

The more we are able to specialize and to maximize our comparative advantage in a particular sphere, the more compartmentalized our lives become. All of these trends are encompassed in our conventional view of modernization and development. For modernization and development are not simply matters of ever-increasing GNP. They are also the reorganization of society along industrial and commercial lines, and in the conventional view represent the essential processes for growth. "Modernization" also means new social relationships, new property relations and new ways of organizing work in place of the old ones, as surely as it means more goods. And if we see no other goals in life but modernization and development, it follows that because commercial relations and industrial organization are more efficient and productive, they ought to expand into more spheres of our life. This is the logical conclusion to formal economic processes.

CHAPTER THREE

THE NATURE OF INFORMAL ECONOMIC ACTIVITY

In recent years, growing attention has been drawn to the phenomenon of the "informal economy." That term has come to have several different, and sometimes contradictory, uses and meanings. We will therefore begin by showing briefly how others have characterized the informal economy.

Pre- or non-industrial economies. Examples of these in Canada include small-scale agriculture and fisheries and the hunting and trapping economies of Indians and Inuit in the North. (See Appendix B.) The term is also used with respect to peasant agriculture and to the self-employed producers and distributors in the cities of the Third World.[1] There are two key features of this kind of economic activity. One is that it is based on self-employment--or what is sometimes called petty commodity production--rather than wage employment.[2] Production is undertaken by small units, usually organized along family and kinship lines, which own (or have use rights to) their own means of production: tools, buildings and land. Whatever they produce beyond their domestic needs they exchange or sell, usually in a local market or to a merchant trader. The other feature of a pre- or non-industrial economy is that it is typically found in small, rural or isolated communities with very limited but highly influential linkages to the world economy.

Although it is commonly supposed that all types of family-based enterprises (like the family farm) are doomed to disappear in the wake of progress, there is considerable evidence that this is not necessarily so and that self-employment and non-monetized exchange may to some extent reclaim certain areas of the economy.

The household economy.   This is the "original" economy in the sense that the Greek roots of the word economy meant household management.   Modern economic theory views the household as the sphere of consumption, rather than production. (See Appendix A.) Nonetheless, the household clearly engages in productive economic activity which results in goods and services for itself and, in some cases, for others.   For the most part, however, these goods and services are for the internal consumption of the household.   The domestic or household economy produces by far the greatest part of the entire national output of child care and household care.   As well, and as we see in Chapter Five, some households are partly or largely self-sufficient in such things as food, clothing and energy production, or the maintenance and renovation of the basic capital stock of shelter, transport and appliances.

The neighborhood or mutual-aid economy.   This is an extension of the domestic economy of the household.[3]   Where there are well-established links among households--for example, in small communities, stable urban neighborhoods or among extended kin (especially those living in close proximity)--goods and services may be produced through cooperation.   These households may exchange the goods and services among themselves, commonly on a non-monetized or non-commercial basis, or people may volunteer their time in community or cooperative activities. In doing so, the volunteers provide goods and services which are needed locally, if not by the donor's household then by other households in the community.

The alternative or counterculture economy.   This includes a broad spectrum of activities, most of which tend to exist in opposition to their social environment rather than as an integral feature of it.   Examples of where this type of economy can be found include land-based religious orders, traditional agricultural sects (such as the Amish or Hutterites, utopian or so-called "intentional" communities) and the ex-urbanite "back to the land" movement.   Some of these have a strong communal focus, while others are much more individualistic in motivation, involving single households.

The common threads are a rejection of mainstream values, an emphasis on simplicity--whether in technology, consumption, organization or the pace of life--and the ideal of self-sufficiency.[4] In the more individualistic examples, people choose such a way of life rather than being born into it. Even in the case of agrarian sects, because they exist in contrast to the social milieu, each generation must reaffirm its commitment. Consequently, there is a tendency for such communities to be inward-looking and preoccupied with. survival. In the case of some religious orders, there is no biological maintenance of membership. Although each of these forms faces certain unusual problems in maintaining or reproducing itself over time, such communities do in fact continue to exist and to reappear.

Small enterprise. Another commonly identified feature of the informal economy is the small scale of its operations. "Small is Beautiful" is a phrase now well known far beyond the actual readership of E.F. Schumacher's book.[5] In Eastern Europe, the informal economy is conceived to be a small-scale market enterprise sector which would be free of the rigidities of state enterprise.

The focus in small enterprises is on flexibility, informality and individual initiative, which are the hallmarks of small business as opposed to the bureaucracy of large corporations. The scale of operation varies from the smallholder--such as the owner-operated farm or business or self-employed craftsperson--to manufacturing and commercial enterprises which, although employing dozens of people and grossing millions of dollars, are commonly classed as small businesses. In practice, these represent a very broad spectrum containing much diversity of purpose and interest.

Some small enterprises are in this category only because they have not yet grown large. Others are established with no intent of getting larger. Individuals or partners may seek no more than to serve a very local or specialized need. They may seek only to follow a dream: incorporation as a small business is a purely technical device with no intention of making money beyond the needs of the enterprise and a decent living for one's self. Usually, however, proprietors have a very strong commitment to the enterprise, a commitment they often expect the employees to share. The relationship between owner and employees may be egalitarian, paternalistic or authoritarian--there is no inevitable pattern. Whatever the particular situation, however, certain features of the formal economy are present: certainly, the use of money as a means of exchange; some standard accounting and business practices (including contractual arrangements); and probably the accumulation of capital and a hierarchical structure of management.

The black, underground or hidden economy. These terms are used to describe a range of economic activity, from the obviously criminal through that which contravenes civil statutes or regulations, up to activity which (although not illegal) the parties choose to keep unrecorded for whatever reason. Organized drug trafficking, prostitution and pornography are economic activities which are concealed for obvious reasons. So are embezzlement, corporate fraud, petty pilfering on the job and the unauthorized use of employment insurance or social assistance payments.

A somewhat different case is activity which in itself is perfectly legal, but is concealed to facilitate tax avoidance or evasion. This too occurs at all levels--from creative bookkeeping on the part of large corporations, to small tradespeople discounting for unreceipted cash payments, to ignoring sales tax at the neighborhood garage sale.

Finally, the underground economy encompasses unrecorded employment, generally in the least skilled and lowest paid sectors. Examples are the employment of immigrant labor--legally or illegally in the country--as domestics, as seasonal farm laborers and in sweat shops. Another example is the modern equivalent of the putting-out system or cottage industry--piece work at home, home distributorships and the like--in which people are nominally self-employed but do not, in fact, own any means of production. In these situations, employers are merely reducing their costs and responsibilities by circumventing the minimum wage, the labor code, payroll deductions, employee benefits and labor unions (and, in some cases, even the need to provide a workplace).[6] Very often these practices are perpetuated by intimidation, poverty and ignorance.

There is no single theme, motivation or value which typifies underground activities. Some are undertaken to make vast profits in the full knowledge that they are illegal. Some are concealed because, while not strictly illegal, there is widespread disapproval of them. Some are simply unrecorded because people are unaware of the requirement to do so. In some cases, people simply wish to avoid red tape and inconvenience in doing what they have always done and feel no need to apologize to anyone for continuing to do so. This last reason is especially the case when employers, financial institutions or the state formalize activities which have previously been informal.

The fact that none of these activities are properly accounted for in the gross national product (GNP) does not of itself make them informal. Instead, they are illegal or quasi-legal forms of economic activities which otherwise range from the most formal to the most informal. For that reason, we reject the underground economy as a subset of the informal economy. Rather it underlies the entire economy, formal and informal.

To economists and policy makers attempting to measure and guide the overall economy, it may make little economic difference whether unrecorded, hidden or invisible economic activity is legal or illegal. Unrecorded, but legal informal activity, can be mixed in with unrecorded underground or illegal activity. The end result is that gross national product and employment totals are incomplete: some activity is not being recorded. However, from our standpoint there is a big difference between legal (informal) and illegal (underground) economic activity. Because we are only interested in encouraging legitimate informal economic activity, we therefore address the underground economy very little. We have included some estimates of its size in Chapter Five.

The policy prescriptions for underground income activities are non-economic and uncomplicated. Illegal activities could, if authorities wished, be more tightly controlled through more vigilant policing efforts. Similarly, significant amounts of undeclared income could, if authorities wished, be uncovered by taxation officials.

Some General Observations on the Informal Economy

There are similarities which emerge from the six forms of informal economic activity described above, except to some extent the last. Many of these similarities were discussed during an international seminar on the informal economy sponsored by the Vanier Institute of the Family in 1979. The informal economy:

- "embraces those parts of the economy in which goods and services are exchanged informally and without money transactions or, when money is involved, it is to provide sustenance and not to increase profits ... the will to accumulate capital for its own sake is not present."
- "is unquantified, unrecorded, uncounted and often even invisible. It includes the activities that men, women and children perform to make their homes and communities more satisfying places ... [and] ... work that people do for one another in the community ... without exchanging

money."
- includes "some but not all self-employed people; many but not all community, non-profit enterprises; most voluntary groups . . ; neighbourly cooperation, whether among people who opt out of the mainstream . . . or among cultural groups . . . [who practice it] . . . as an inherited way of life; trading, bartering and exchanging goods and services with neighbours . . . [and] . . . household activities; meal preparation, laundering, care of children . . ."
- embodies, both in practice and as value preferences, such patterns as neighborly cooperation, sharing, mutual aid and support, local autonomy and self-reliance, material simplicity, trust, sensitivity, diversity, participation and the decentralization of power, in contrast to the formal economy which in certain respects tends to promote the opposite characteristics.[7]

The Essence of the Informal Economy

Many of the above characterizations are useful, although in our view they do not go far enough and no one of them tells the whole story. Much of what we say in this book about the informal economy has been said before, but in bits and pieces. When identifying a "new" phenomenon that we do not know much about, it is frequently practical to describe it in terms of what we do know, which in this case is the formal economy.

It is at first tempting to define the informal economy as simply the opposite of the formal economy, but on the closer inspection this leads to confusion. We might suppose, for example, that in the informal economy there is neither commerce nor industry, money nor capital. We might even imagine that contractual arrangements are unnecessary because anonymity is replaced by engagement and commitment, self-interest by altruism and trust, competition by cooperation and hierarchy and authority by consensus and egalitarianism. Perhaps in the informal economy everyone can be a shepherd in the morning and a philosopher in the afternoon, as Karl Marx envisaged, and alienation can be eliminated by true human community. The informal economy would, in short, be an economy in which everyone is happy and nice to one another. Indeed, this is how some people romanticize traditional Indian and Inuit life--and even the rural Canadian life of a couple of generations ago.

The problem is that when the informal economy is so defined, it is an entirely imaginary and utopian economy which tells us nothing about real life. If there is a common theme to all the variations of informal economy that have been identified (save the underground or black economy), it is that they are *familiar* economies. In them, the participants know one another or of one another. The informal economy is the economy of a small society, in contrast to that of a mass society. This means above all that the informal economy is organized in small economic units in which the objective of maximizing either profits or utilities does not and cannot exist apart from the goal of maintaining the mutual social bonds and obligations of the local society.

The concept of the informal economy as the familiar economy should put to rest the more romantic and utopian views of it. After all, it has been commonly observed that familiarity breeds contempt. Because people know one another does not necessarily mean they like one another. Recent Canadian crime statistics indicate that about 80 percent of homicide victims die at the hands of family, friends and associates, not strangers. Life in a large extended family or in a small community can be nurturing and fulfilling, but it can also be oppressive and stifling. Exploitation and brutality are by no means absent from family and community.

Nonetheless, the informal economy meets essential human needs that the formal economy does not and cannot meet. For most people, formal economic relationships do not involve commitment, engagement, cooperation or intimacy. Many people do not find self-sufficiency, creativity, autonomy, integration and diversity in their working lives. And many are unable to find stability, security, control or prestige in their formal economic relations. The fact that for some people the very opposite is true--the formal economy meets deeply felt needs that family and neighborhood cannot meet--does not negate the importance of the informal economy. It simply means that people need both economies, and that an important goal of public policy should be the provision of a mix from which individuals can choose what best meets their needs.

Where do we find examples of informal economic activity? In Chapter Four, we describe the spheres of life in which the informal economy is important and the structure and institutions that typify these spheres. As well, in Appendix B, we provide a description of what might be thought of as a model or archetype of the informal economy: what we call the "village economy," as typified by many northern and rural Canadian communities. The purpose of this description is not to idealize the village economy (although we find many worthy things about it), but rather to highlight from a simple example what is more difficult to identify in a complex urban society. As well, we identify in Appendix B some of the major forces from the external formal economy that are changing the village economy and how people are responding to these changes.

What follows is a more generalized account of the informal economy, based on the structures described in Chapter Four and Appendix B.

Informal Economic Units

One of the key features of informal economic activity is that the economic units--the groups that produce and consume-- are small. When we look at how these units--whether they are households or even larger groups which are based on neighborhood and mutual interests--operate economically, we see a complex mix of activities and functions. The catalogue of polar opposites --production and consumption, market and non-market, economic and social, work and leisure--that typifies the formal economy is much less evident. For example, it would be impossible to find a purely domestic economic unit in real life, producing all it consumes and consuming all it produces. We like to romanticize that the pioneer family farm or the Indian or Inuit household of earlier days were like this, but they never were. They not only depended on broad networks of mutual aid and sharing within the community but also on some type of long-distance commercial trade.

Agriculture, fisheries and trapping in Canada were always organized for production for far-away markets as well as for domestic consumption. This combination of domestic and commercial production is still familiar to hundreds of thousands of Canadian households. It extends to distribution as well as production--for example, the small corner storekeeper, who having purchased an inventory of goods, sells much of it but keeps some for his family, thus obtaining his domestic food supply at wholesale prices. Like many small-scale producers he has chosen to retain the value potentially added by his labor rather than exchange it in the market.

Not all household units of production combine domestic and exchange activities in this way. An example of one that exchanges all it produces and produces nothing it consumes would be a large family-owned and -operated grain farm, where not even a kitchen garden is maintained. It might be, however, that this farm is incorporated, employs hired help and has such a heavy reliance on large capital assets (financed chiefly by bank loans) that we would have great difficulty distinguishing it from a small firm in its behavior.

Short of this extreme, however, are certain features which all "household"-producing units share and which distinguish them from the firm, in its ideal form, and from the formal economy. This type of small unit is not always a household; it may be, in legal form, an unincorporated business, a partnership, a voluntary organization, a cooperative or a small community development corporation. Whatever its form, it is owner-operated. These informal (or less formal) units are more similar to households than to firms in their internal organization of work and in their internal social relationships. Further, there is an important relationship to the local community which affects the rationale and style of operation.

The informal unit typically has substantial ownership rights over whatever it needs in order to produce things--buildings, tools, machinery, vehicles, raw materials and so on. It may own some of these things outright, it may rent or lease some or it may finance their purchase by borrowing money. These different arrangements will result in varying degrees of internal control over the productive operation. Outright ownership will allow a much more informal manner of operation. Heavy indebtedness to lending institutions or certain types of franchise arrangements, on the other hand, leave very little room for autonomy.[8]

Farmers who have purchased (rather than inherited) their lands, equipment and stock, or "independent" truckers who have purchased their tractor-trailers and whose indebtedness runs to five or six figures, have their operations closely supervised by creditors. Such enterprises run a substantial risk of losing their productive assets if they do not meet the creditor's conditions. Similarly, a franchised business like a gas station or a fast food outlet must conform to a long list of operating standards. To run a McDonald's franchise, you have to go to Hamburger University to learn not so much how to run *a* business as how to run *theirs*. The American dream of independence through having a small business is thus, in some cases, little more than a sham, where the operator assumes the risk and the financier or franchiser controls the use of the business.

Productive facilities that are owned more or less outright by informal units, however, are less likely to be run in the manner of the firm. The owners' goals are much more likely to involve maintenance and survival than accumulation and growth. Many small enterprises are established simply to meet a local need, or to help fulfill the owner's dream about doing something, rather than to make big money. The owners do not intend for the business to grow beyond a certain point, and have no inclination to amass great profits beyond the needs of maintaining the enterprise in a steady and viable state.

One of the distinctive features of informal units is that owners, managers and workers are very often the same people. They do not think of their own labor as a commodity separate from, let alone in opposition to, their capital assets or their managerial capacities. They are their own bosses. It is common for farmers, small businesspeople and freelance professionals or tradespeople to work long hours and to put a lot of their income back into their businesses.[9]

The Rationale of Informal Economics

The industrial pattern of work is largely absent from the informal economy. During certain times or seasons, the hours may be long and the pace strenuous, while at other times, one can go fishing or read a novel. In neither case is there any need to clock in, or to be on the job merely for the sake of filling a chair. Self-employed producers neither limit nor force themselves to work an eight-hour day or a five-day week. They do whatever has, in their judgement, to be done without thought of overtime, sick leave or holidays. The total hours of work over a year may be much greater than their industrial counterpart's and their "pay" less (insofar as that can even be calculated), but they decide their time and pace of work. If they like what they do, they make no clear distinction between work and leisure because when they are not physically working, they may be thinking about it or doing something related to it.

Where two or more people are involved as co-producers in a small enterprise, they likely share values and approaches to their work and make mutually satisfactory arrangements among themselves about the organization of work. Contrary to industrial practice, people in informal units are unlikely to either compel others to take risks with their health and safety or induce them to do so with the offer of high reward. This does not mean that there is no risk in such operations. On the contrary, it is well known that such occupations as farming, fishing and certain crafts or trades have high health and safety risks. These risks, however, are shared equally among co-producers who are free to take whatever safety precautions they as individuals or as a group see fit.

Most small enterprises and organizations have the choice of consuming, selling or reinvesting the goods and services they produce. Farmers can eat, sell or keep their animals for breeding, and commonly do all three in some proportion. Fishermen can eat or sell their fish, corner grocers can eat or sell their inventories and carpenters can build their own houses as well as someone else's. These are all "entrepreneurial" or management decisions on a small scale. The people who make them consider a wide variety of factors--tradition, market prices, wage rates, the opportunity cost of domestic consumption.[10] Not only is there a choice to keep or sell one's own produce but very often also the choice of working for wages.

Thus, we find that farmers, fishermen, artisans and independent tradespeople may also, from time to time, take outside jobs. This is usually a temporary strategy, with the main objective being to maintain one's status as an independent producer. Similarly, where these are household rather than individual strategies, one adult may work full time as an independent producer and another as a full-time wage employee. This is especially common in rural areas.

Wherever low capitalization is required, there is likely to be a more flexible strategy of moving between independent production and wage employment, as need or choice dictates. Where somewhat greater levels of capitalization are required, these may be financed out of savings from wage earnings, either as a "nest egg" in advance or continuously from the employment of one or more household members. For example, over one-third of Canadian farmers are part-time operators, and an unknown but higher percentage of Canadian farm households rely on off-farm income.[11]

We have all heard of the disappearing family farm. Agriculture, like other primary occupations, is commonly thought of as a declining sector in terms of employment. From an allegedly backward and traditional reserve of small producers emerge a few modern, industrial, commercial farm businesses, and those unable to compete leave for the city. A recent study of agricultural census returns, however, has shown that entry into and exit from agriculture is more flexible than gross figures on the decline of the number of farms would indicate.[12] Thirty percent of 1976 farm operators had entered farming during the previous ten years, while the same percentage of farmers during the years 1966 to 1976 had operated continuously throughout the decade. This research further suggested a growing distinction between full-time, commercial farmers (owners of agribusinesses) and part-time smallholders. Only a relatively small proportion of the former category got into or out of their operations by means of part-time farming combined with outside wage employment.

Patterns of consumption and investment are also quite different for independent producers. For the wage earner, income accrues on a regular, frequent and predictable basis, but almost all of it is required for current expenditure on daily subsistence and time payments. The purchase of large items must be financed on a long and sustained basis of savings or of debt repayment. These big ticket items are, however, considered by economists and tax collectors to be consumer rather than producer goods, even though they may include the tools and appliances by which people provide meals, shelter, heat, clothing, transport and other useful items for themselves and others on a domestic basis. (This is one of the practical consequences of excluding the ordinary business of providing for household needs from the concept of work.) For the wage earner, consumption is finely tuned to a more or less predictable flow of income. The purchase of large items is based not simply on total price, but on projected monthly payments. "Can we afford it?" means can we sustain this additional level of monthly expenditure for the next two to five years.

For independent producers however, income frequently accrues in large seasonal or sporadic lump sums, whose amounts are only roughly predictable. However, since daily household needs are in part met from domestic production, much of these lump sums can be used for the purchase of big ticket items without resort to short-term loans at high interest rates. There is often a tendency to gear the level of commodity production or the length of casual wage employment to specific targets--to earn enough to buy a particular item and then quit.

A key feature of informal activity is its extension beyond the family or household into the local community. Where the tradition is strong--and this appears to be in both rural and urban areas with stable populations--there tends to be a strong egalitarian ethic and sense of community. Personal responsibility and self-reliance in certain spheres of life are combined with mutual aid and cooperation in others. There are well-developed community institutions that take responsibility for local social and economic welfare, although since the 1940s these have been replaced to some extent by a centralized system of redistribution of income and delivery of social services.

The quality of the produce, the well-being of the producer, stewardship of land and resources and the aesthetics of production are community as well as individual concerns. Where the sense of community is strong, there are more likely to be high standards in these areas. Those standards exist apart from, or in addition to, standards which the market might impose. The concerns for the local community separate the informal economic unit from certain types of small businesses whose operations are entirely divorced from the surrounding community's economic structure. These businesses are likely to operate secretively, to sell their entire output in an anonymous and far-distant market and to freely relocate at their convenience.

What is important here is the environment in which the economic unit functions. Informal economic units operating in a community context will behave differently from firms operating in a competitive market. This distinction is much more important than the legal niceties of ownership. For example, there are many publicly owned firms in Canada, but their operating style is rarely distinguishable from that of privately owned firms-- consider Air Canada and CP Air.

The paramount objectives of the firm in a competitive market--the criteria by which we measure its performance--are capital accumulation, profitability, productivity, efficiency and control. These are all reducible to simple measures of profit and loss--the bottom line. In an informal environment, the economic unit tends to value maintenance and long-run survival over growth and short-run profits.

Does this mean that the unit of production in an informal environment is not governed at all by what everyone understands to be the basic rules of economics? Not at all. It has no less interest in economizing--trying to get a greater return for less effort--than does the firm. Any small productive unit--household or other--must be efficient in its work methods, use its resources wisely, be able to keep production and consumption in balance and keep its environment fit for life. All social systems--all the units that make them up and all the individuals within them--try to economize, from the simplest hunting society to the most complex industrial system, whether organized along capitalist or socialist lines.

Some argue that capitalism and industrialization represent the most logical and successful institutionalization of this "natural" tendency. Without attempting to compare social systems, what we are suggesting here is that capitalism (whose functions are effected primarily through the formal economy) does this at the expense of other important values, which represent equally "natural" human tendencies, and that the informal economy incorporates these other values in its rationality to a much greater degree than does the formal. It should be added that industrial socialism, to the extent that it tries to mimic industrial capitalism, also ignores informal values, and at the same time leaves fewer legal niches in the system for the independent producer and for the informal economy.

The difference between the formal and informal environments is that, whereas the firm maximizes for a very few variables and is content to ignore other variables as beyond its scope and responsibility, the informal unit tries to maximize for both more variables and more people. The importance of community institutions and control is that the individual units cannot ignore their "externalities"--their waste, noise and pollution; their aggressive, selfish and uncooperative behavior; their appropriation of limited resources at other's expense. Where the commercial market rewards greed and aggression, the community restrains these tendencies.

Operating in Two Environments

No one in our society can live exclusively in an informal economic environment, and indeed few want to. As Appendix B illustrates, even in rural and remote communities the formal economy is very much a part of life, and everyone must make choices between the two. The kinds of decisions that informal economic units must make about domestic or commercial production and consumption also face the ordinary Canadian household.

Do we eat at home or at a restaurant? Do we grow a garden or buy everything at the grocery store? Do we put up food and make our own clothes or buy these things? Do we renovate our own house or hire a contractor? Fix the car ourselves or take it to the garage? Arrange our work lives to share looking after the children or put them in day care? Have our aging parents nearby or in an old folks' home?

And if we decide to go the informal route instead of buying and hiring, in what quantities do we make these things or provide these services? Do we produce just enough for ourselves, a little extra to share or exchange with family and neighbors or a lot extra to sell to others on a more commercial basis? And how shall we juggle all these activities with our need, economic or otherwise, to be involved with the formal economy--to hold down a job or run a farm or business?

While most Canadians do not make these decisions in the context of an encompassing village economy, neither are these decisions purely economic in nature. Matters of personal status and enjoyment are also at stake. Some people are willing to spend practically as much or more on day care, housecleaning and restaurant meals as they make at work, because they like the social involvement and intellectual stimulation that their jobs provide. Some people do not like their jobs very much, but like the status that comes with money--the power to buy other peoples' labor to get things done, instead of having to do the jobs themselves.

Some people feel that with only so much time in the day there are certain services they would rather purchase than provide for themselves, even if they are capable of doing so and sometimes enjoy doing so. Others feel that the satisfactions derived from being self-sufficient or self-reliant, from working as a family unit or from working cooperatively and voluntarily with neighbors and friends, surpass the importance of any monetary savings in doing these things or of doing other things with their time.

But just as individuals must operate in both the formal and informal economies, so too do informal economic units have to operate in both a community and a competitive market environment. Consequently, the problem of seeking and maintaining a balance among objectives, with limited time and resources, is as great for the self-employed individual, for the co-op, the collective or the non-profit operation as it is for individual members of the household.

Both environments are essential in our society, and the problem is how to maintain each without disrupting or undermining the other. There is no doubt that the growth of industry and commerce has so far been at the expense of the informal economy, and that whether through necessity or choice, most Canadian households and other informal economic units have come to rely more heavily on the formal economy. Should we assume that it is either inevitable or desirable that this shift from informal to formal continue indefinitely? What would it be like if informal economic activity were completely displaced from every corner of our society?

The simplistic view of modernization and progress suggests that more is better, that it is human nature to willingly trade any and all parts of one's heritage and way of life for more goodies and that only industrial civilization can bring these goodies.

It is certainly true that people like the goodies. Very rarely do we observe individuals, let alone whole communities, conciously and deliberately rejecting them. It does not follow, however, that people have fully understood and accepted the changes which are required in their social organization--the organization of work, the system of property rights and the mutual rights and obligations among kin and community--all changes that the continued production of these goodies seems to entail.

In recent years, there has been an unprecedented level of concern with the impact of development--both social and environmental. This is surely the sign of a growing public recognition that modernization has exacted a heavy price and that we did not in the outcome obtain the goodies for nothing. Wherever people have risen to the defense of their community, the struggle has been about more than a piece of land or property or levels of income.

It is also a defense of a way of life that can only be sustained by a community of people--a way of life that is not just a combination of interchangeable factors of production, and which loses much of its meaning and force when practiced individually rather than collectively.

Contrasting Formal and Informal Economies

What we are suggesting is that the formal and informal economies can best be distinguished by the structural or institutional relationships they engender among people. These are relative differences or tendencies, however, rather than mutual opposites. It cannot be said that the formal economy is marked by the invariable presence of some characteristics, while the informal economy is marked by their complete absence.

For example, markets exist in the informal economy, but they are very limited in scope. The factors of supply, demand and consumer choice govern the operation of a garage sale in many of the same ways they govern the supermarket. But not everything is a commodity in the informal economy. Within the household, for example, it would not occur to us to sell food to the highest bidder and let others go hungry. Instead, we make sure everybody is fed whatever is available. We do not withold affection or consolation from friends or family because they have not paid their insurance premiums. Friends and neighbors normally exchange tools, help or baby-sitting services without writing up a bill for the exact amount and without cash payment. The absence of money exchange does not mean that people fail to evaluate what is being exchanged, however. It means only that the balance and reciprocity which are expected will occur over a long period of time, that the exchange involves aspects of the relationship which are not readily quantifiable and that there will be a generous allowance for particular circumstances. Very seldom are goods and services given freely with no expectation of return. Nor do we consider the industrial relations model very appropriate for organizing work in the home or neighborhood. So the market, industrial organization and money are largely, but not entirely, absent from the informal economy.

In the same way, informal economic relations tend to be the opposite of market and industrial relations. We do not normally have contracts in the informal economy, although one could point to the increasing use of formal legal contracts in family (particularly marital) arrangements. Instead, we rely more on trust. This trust is based on knowledge and experience of the people with whom we are dealing--their reliability and loyalty, the likelihood that they will still be around next month and next year and what social pressures are on them to fulfill their stated (or unstated) obligations. When there is a broad range of common understanding, expectation and mutual obligation among people, it does not occur to us to write up a contract to cover every transaction.

We do not normally operate in a social Darwinist, self-defense style within the household or the neighborhood. Most would think it peculiar, not to say reprehensible, to be constantly suspicious of our family and friends and always trying to get the jump on them. We do not normally think of the family or the neighborhood as a zero-sum economy, where for every winner there is a loser. The informal economy relies primarily on cooperation, solidarity, mutual aid and consensus.

In contrast to industrial life, the informal economy is marked by substantial flexibility and by generalized rather than specialized competence. The greater the reliance on the informal economy, the greater the variety of useful everyday skills people will have. These not only include technical abilities--food storage and preparation, gardening, mechanical repairs, household renovations and sewing--but also social and organizational skills to ensure that within the relevant group, work gets done, things get distributed and people get taken care of. The sheer variety of things to be done requires greater role flexibility, that is, the ability of people to fill in for others as necessary. The skills and attitudes necessary for work in the informal economy are normally transmitted within the family and the community, rather than through formal institutions like the schools.

The informal economy is a highly decentralized economy. Whereas there are about three-quarters of a million firms in Canada of which about 2 percent produce almost half the country's total value of goods and services, there are 9 million households in the country whose domestic output is spread much more evenly. In the informal economy of our households and neighborhoods, we know who is responsible for what and what to expect of them. We can talk to those people and make our feelings known to them. This does not, of course, mean that we necessarily like what every one of them does. Yet, because the power of any one of those people is limited, we can each devise strategies of counteraction or avoidance which minimize the impact of such individuals upon ourselves. In the informal economy, no single large and powerful economic unit can suddenly overturn our lives by closing its doors, by changing its product, price or purchasing policy without notice--or by expropriating the neighborhood.

There are, of course, families and communities where these

qualities are not so evident. And there are large economic organizations and corporations which try to introduce at least some of these informal qualities into their methods and organization of production. The corporation cannot be all-inclusive, however, in the way that the household and the community can be. Whatever claim corporations may make about being like families or communities, the inescapable fact is that in corporations, people are expendable for economic reasons. Those laid off, and thus excluded from the corporate collectivity, are left to their own devices or to the generosity of other institutions in society. While people can also get excluded from their family and community, this is normally a very drastic step, likely to occur for other than economic reasons.

Perhaps the least clearcut difference between the formal and informal economies is the matter of hierarchy and authority. Many households operate along lines just as authoritarian and paternalistic as the formal economy. Many formal economic institutions, and these types of families themselves, consider their operating methods to be good training for the formal economy. Another such area is in the matter of work roles. In the informal economy, as in more traditional economies, the division of labor is primarily sexual. Despite the rise of feminism in recent years, Chapter Five shows that there is still a heavy burden on women with respect to housekeeping and child care. Many households are marked by as rigid a division of labor as any large factory or construction project with multiple union jurisdictions.

In general, however, informal economic institutions are based on the engagement of people rather than people's anonymity. These institutions are based on the assumption that people know one another and are willing to make allowances for individual capacities or incapacities. These are not institutions for strangers. So there is a much more holistic and less fragmented and compartmentalized view of what is going on and what respective roles are. Price becomes one of the least important pieces of information in informal economic relationships.

In the informal economy, instead of doing ultraspecialized jobs making parts and components of incomplete things for unknown destinations, "whole" jobs are undertaken for people known and depended upon. And because work and produce tend to be performed and distributed locally--and the effects of the enterprise felt locally--there is much more understanding and involvement in and control over what is going on. Self-reliance, familiar traditions and institutions and personal perceptions and common sense are the norm, rather than dependence on experts with incomprehensible skills, on studies with unfamiliar techniques and on distant authorities with uncertain purposes and commitments.

An important difference between formal and informal economic relations is the role of time in each. Informal relations require a substantial amount of time to create and solidify. They arise from sustained membership over many years in a community of people--whether based on kinship, neighborhood or mutual interest--so that we can, in fact, know the personal qualities and what to expect of one another. In any society, this knowledge becomes codified after a period of time. Status exists in informal economies, just as it does in traditional societies, and in both cases is, in part, a substitute for time. By knowing someone's status or relationship to ourselves, we know immediately much of what is appropriate and expected behavior between us. But in all small groups, status is tempered by actual performance.

In a mass society, formal economic institutions serve the very important purpose of codifying behavior and expectations among perfect strangers. There are many transactions in modern life in which we cannot possibly judge the outcome on the basis of the personal qualities of the people involved, because we cannot possibly know all the people involved.

If you wish to fly overseas, for example, there is no possible way of knowing all those who made the aircraft, run the airlines, control the flights and handle the baggage, so as to judge their personal competence and reliability. Informal economic institutions and relations are unable to provide adequate assurance of your safety and comfort in this situation. So it is most appropriate that there are formal economic arrangements for this purpose--international standards of aircraft construction and operating procedures, precise flight schedules, contractual agreements (about what you are entitled to expect for your purchase of an airline ticket) and so on.

Formal, anonymous economic relations are a substitute (often a necessary one) for the time which is required to build informal economic relations. Purely formal relations are, in fact, solely economic: we judge the merits of each transaction on the basis of its immediate economic utility and value to us, as the phrase "cash and carry" so neatly suggests. Informal relations are, however, social as well as economic and we would have great difficulty dissociating the two. Informal relations harmonize the much longer-run basis of economic well-being--balanced and generalized reciprocity--with genuine affection, liking, loyalty and altruism. In real life, of course, there is some blending of formal and informal relations across the entire spectrum of our activities. If we work in a large corporate factory or bureaucratic office for any length of time, we may develop close personal relations with co-workers which will temper our otherwise purely "economic" behavior. Professional and managerial people intertwine business and personal relationships quite closely over their careers; personal friendships and family relations count along with individual merit and qualifications in getting things done.

It is nonetheless true that there is a strong tendency in the formal economy to save time, to focus effort on narrowly conceived goals, to value output over process and to eliminate the "non-economic" aspects of our work--to get the job done and go on to something else. In the informal economy, we are more likely to value the activity as an end in itself, as well as a means to produce something else. Working relations are social relations. We feel no need to sacrifice the personal and the unique. We can savor time instead of saving it.

In the formal economy, time is a cost and also includes risk (for example, in dealing with strangers). These are accounted for by interest rates and payments which vary according to the extent of said time and risk. In the informal economy, however, there is little or no resort to interest rates. Where there is balanced reciprocity in a community, it means that if one person loans another a tool or helps someone for a day or two with a building or a garden, there is the expectation that similar aid will be forthcoming in return at some future time. This aid might come from the particular individual helped or from other members of the community, but it is not a repayment in a precise amount at a precise time by a particular person. Rather it is a mutual understanding that by having contributed to the well-being of other individuals or groups, however defined, there is a claim on time and goods when needed. As community or family members, we do not expect to be paid back with interest because we do not perceive any significant risk of not being repaid, however long or circuitous the route might be. Over the generational cycle, parents care for their children and years later children take care of their parents. If interest were added on to this example of balanced reciprocity, the burden on each succeeding generation would become astronomical (especially at current rates)! Thus, there is a built-in inflationary factor in the formal economy which does not apply in the informal sector.

Time matters in the informal economy insofar as its efficient use means more work gets done with less effort. In the formal economy, however, time has an additional and crucial dimension: it relates to capital as well as to labor. Saving time becomes chiefly a means of using capital more efficiently. And the greater the proportion of capital in the enterprise, the more it seems that human purposes are subordinated to the needs of capital. Since productive units in the formal economy tend to be much more heavily capitalized than in the informal, the demands of capital on time are much greater in the former.

Ironically, although future benefits are discounted at a much greater rate in the formal than in the informal economy, the long-term consequences of decision making in the formal economy are substantially greater, and much less easily prevented and reversed. Major industrial innovation and retooling and megaproject developments are examples where decisions taken today commit vast amounts of energy and capital for many years ahead. If public perception of the benefits of the developments changes over time, or unforeseen adverse consequences arise, the commitment to the time and capital already invested weighs heavily against changes and redirections. For example, in the formal economy the major sources of toxic waste in concentrations overburdensome to air, water and soil are the large-scale, heavy extractive and processing industries. The unwillingness of any industrialized society--capitalist or socialist--to change the output of its central investments is all too obvious.

By contrast, in the informal economy individual errors and misjudgements are more easily counterbalanced by the success of myriad other households and enterprises. It may not be any easier for an individual or a small enterprise to cut one's losses and walk away from a mistake, but the consequences to others of not doing so are much more limited. The informal economy tends to use more labor and more time, less energy, fewer resources, less capital, and to have less (or certainly less sudden) environmental impact. Productivity, as measured by output per unit of labor time, is greater in the formal economy, or at least certain sectors of it. But if there is a long-term trend towards capital, energy and resources becoming more expensive relative to the cost of labor, then production in the informal sector gains in comparative advantage.

Figure 1 shows the general societal shift from the informal to the formal economy. The diagram is, of course, only a hypothetical representation as there are no standardized empirical measurements over time of the mix of formal and informal activity or output.

FIGURE I

The Changing Mix of Formal and Informal Activity Over Time

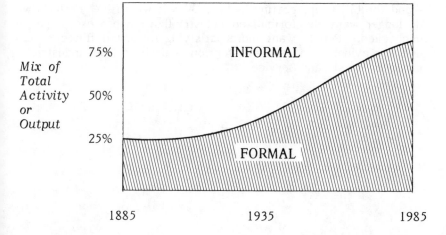

A century ago, a much higher proportion of our total economic output was derived from the informal economy. This shift is also associated with the transformation from a rural agricultural economy (and in the North, a hunting and gathering society) to an urban industrial one. We commonly think of that process as modernization and the result as economic development. Conventional economic development theory claims that any substantial increase in national and per capita output requires a shift from informal to formal economic relations--that contracts, individualism, mobility, centralization and specialization should replace kinship and status, solidarity, stability, the local community and integration. According to conventional theory, a primary position must be allocated to the key institutions of the formal economy: the market, industrial organization and money. Are modernization and progress thus leading inevitably to a complete formalization of the economy? Should they? Are there inherent merits to this process? Is there an optimum balance that we should strive for?

The initial promise and results of industrialization were an incredible supply and variety of goods for the masses at low cost. It seemed that toil and poverty could be eliminated. More recently, the real bill for this cornucopia has been presented: pollution, resource crises, massive unemployment, inflation, unstable communities and households, meaningless jobs, unimaginable poverty in the Third World, complex and remote institutions --and the bill keeps getting higher. Was it worth it? Perhaps we no longer want the formalized industrialization process to go on unchecked. People want more satisfying lives, but it seems less and less evident that this satisfaction is derived from industrially produced goods and services.

CHAPTER FOUR

THE STRUCTURES OF FORMAL AND INFORMAL ECONOMIC ACTIVITY

This chapter provides a more detailed description of the types of structures found in the economy, emphasizing those that embody the essentials of informal activity and have the greatest potential for enhancing and nurturing it. Since conventional economic analysis and policy deal almost exclusively with formal economic structures, the concept of the "whole economy" is used here to designate the total of all economic activity occurring in society. (See Figure 2.)

FIGURE 2

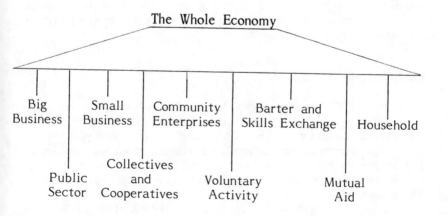

Formal Economic Structures

Big Business

Most people are generally well acquainted with productive activity in the big business sector. When the press, politicians and policy makers talk about the "business" sector or about "big business," it is usually large corporate activity they are referring to. In *Economics and the Public Purpose*, J.K. Galbraith refers to the large corporate sector as the "planning system."[1] The distinction between the planning and market systems is that in the former because economic forces are under tighter control, there is more room for discretionary administrative planning or decision making. Consequently, there is more room and need for bureaucratic, hierarchical organizational structures. On the other hand, small firms in the market system are more controlled by market forces and have little or no discretionary decision-making power and little need for bureaucratic organization. Manpower is very heavily devoted to production, not planning and organizing.

In terms of physical and organizational structure, firms in the big business sector are large employers of usually more than 100 people, but production processes tend to be capital-intensive. With few exceptions, the work force belongs to a large and well-organized union and employee rewards and conditions of work are subject to negotiation. The two principal objectives of large corporate firms are an acceptable-to-maximum level of profits and growth of the enterprise.

Public Sector

The public sector needs little elaboration since its activities are easily recognized and defined by most economic observers. Included in the public sector are employees of all levels of government: federal, provincial, regional and local. Public administrators, teachers in public schools, police officers, public hospital personnel and so on are all considered public employees.

Like the big business sector, the organization of work is carried out along bureaucratic, hierarchical and authoritarian lines. Day-to-day control and decision making are concentrated in the hands of elected officials and senior administrators, such as deputy-ministers, commissioners and board chairpersons. Moreover, control is often further centralized in the hands of senior administrators of central agencies, such as treasury boards, finance commissions, planning and priority setting agencies and so forth. In recent years, employee rewards and conditions have become the subject of negotiations between increasingly strong and well-organized unions and senior management representatives. Monetary rewards, however, very closely reflect the compensation being paid to comparable workers in the big business sector.

Distinct from big business, public sector activity need not be guided by the demands imposed by conditions in the domestic and international marketplace. But very conservative governments often seem to emulate much of the commercial behavior and objectives of large corporations. While the public sector's "bottom line" can be more flexible and attuned to a wider range of human needs, the extent of this depends on the government and administration in power.

Informal Economic Structures

Small Business Enterprises

There are no hard and fast rules for defining small business. But there is a sharp conceptual difference between the enterprise that is fully under the command of an individual and owes its success to this circumstance and the firm which would not exist without organization.[2]

The small business sector more than the big business sector is representative of market or free enterprise economics, where price competition can still be stiff and direct and survival hazardous. Small enterprises seldom enjoy many of the advantages that are conferred upon their large corporate brothers--the luxury of large accumulated profits, restricted competition which allows cost increases to be passed more easily on to the public, access to prime bank rates, large advertising budgets, and open doors to political decision makers and regulatory bodies.

With few employees in each small firm, and with the enterprise frequently owner-managed, there is little need for hierarchical centralized forms of organization and decision making. There is more face-to-face interaction between the employer and employee and often they work side by side. Whether or not the owner-manager consults with or encourages the workers to speak out on the operation of the business is according to the personalities and attitudes of individual owners. But in contrast to the big business and public sectors, the possibility for this kind of small business worker participation always exists since there is much more face-to-face interaction.

Two objectives of traditional small businesses are similar to the big business sector: growth and commercial profit. It is likely, however, that the ranking is reversed with growth being secondary for most small business owners.

Franchised businesses. One form of small business that falls between an individual enterprise and big business is the franchised or leased enterprise. An individual McDonald's hamburger or Shell service station operation is "owned" by the small businessperson, but much control and decision making is in the hands of the parent company or franchise grantor. Franchise and leasing arrangements vary considerably, although it is worth noting that these types of small business operations are frequently nothing more than branch plants of the larger corporate parent.

Family businesses. This type of economic activity can function between two extremes. At one extreme, the family business may operate like a traditional small business with the family head acting as the authoritative owner-employer and other family members being treated as employees within a commercial profit accounting framework. At the other extreme, the business may operate as an economic extension of the family, where decisions are made on a social basis and relationships are along familial rather than employer/employee lines.

In contrast to traditional businesses, an important objective of some family businesses is that they be, in part, an extension of the family life and as much a social as an economic institution. In this context, business and family roles can be difficult to distinguish, whereas in the big business and public sectors private (family) and public (business) roles are quite distinct.

Briarpatch enterprises. The resemblance is very close between this form of economic activity and certain forms of community-owned enterprise. The essential difference is that briarpatch enterprises are initiated and owned privately, either by a person or a small group of people. Briarpatch economic activities are not widely established in Canada, but they represent forms of small business and self-employed activity that could and probably will become attractive alternatives as the formal economy continues its slide.

Briarpatch activities were named after a loose cooperative grouping of about 100 San Francisco "new-age" small businesses. The Briarpatch is a network of small business people who have three values in common: they are doing what they are doing because they enjoy it, they find their major reward in serving people rather than in amassing sums of money, and they share certain resources with one another. Moreover, they keep their books and financial records open to the friends and community members they serve. Briarpatch enterprises are self-sustaining, relying on the sale of their goods and services to the public for their revenue needs. But they manage to retain a social accounting rationale in spite of commercial pressures.

Collective and Cooperative Enterprises

Different enterprises refer to themselves variously as collectives or cooperatives (or cooperative communities). Therefore, we define the two according to how they are most commonly differentiated in practice. It is necessary to keep in mind that public legislation often defines minimum forms, practices and activities to which cooperatives must adhere in order to qualify for advantageous tax and other regulations. Thus, an enterprise may call itself a co-op but not technically be one in the strict legal sense set down by legislation.

Collectives. These enterprises are privately owned by their members like briarpatches, but there is wider ownership. What distinguishes some collectives from "group capitalism" is a strong element of community and social outreach that pervades the goals of the collective. In these types of collectives, commercial profit is secondary. Informally operated collectives may follow fairly traditional business practices and ventures, but then reach out to communities by using their profits to support community groups or activities--women's centers, other collectives, community newspapers and so on. Other collectives may follow much more unconventional and informal business practices, thus accomplishing their social goals directly, for example, by integrating disabled persons into the collective's work force.

From the viewpoint of management and ownership style, collectives can be similar to many community-owned enterprises.

Collectives have a reasonably broad ownership base and decisions are taken collectively through a consensual approach. Collectives may or may not hire employees, but when they do the employees will almost certainly share the general values of the members of the collective. Collectives differ from most community-owned enterprise activities in the source of funding. Whereas collectives get the bulk of their revenue through the sale of their goods and services to the public, usually at full-cost prices, community organizations rely much more heavily on individual, corporate and public grants and donations, with a reduced dependency on proceeds from the sale of their goods and services to the public.

Cooperatives. Cooperatives frequently represent a form of collective. But they must be treated separately because cooperatives can take many forms, often become very large and constitute special legal entities under various public laws. It is also necessary to differentiate between the "cooperative movement" or the spirit of cooperation and the actual cooperative institutions and arrangements which, to varying degrees, put into practice the spirit of cooperation.

In addition to the larger, better known and more formalized co-ops (which on the surface may bear striking resemblances to corporations), there exist smaller cooperative business ventures often requiring considerable member participation in the production process itself. Cooperative day-care centers, food and housing co-ops and cooperative garages are a few of the existing enterprises which frequently require members to directly contribute their time and labor. In these smaller co-ops where membership is limited, each member has a direct voice in the operation. Management style and organizational structure are informal and decisions are often reached by consensus. There may or may not be paid employees, and when there are, they are frequently members of the co-op. These smaller co-ops often operate in a similar manner to collectives.

Although co-ops can be very different, four basic forms can be discerned. While the principles of cooperation are common to each, they are practiced to different degrees.

The *first* form is a cooperative community, sometimes called an intentional community. These co-ops are usually located in rural areas. Members are dedicated to living their whole lives in a cooperative fashion. These communities represent the "purest" application of the principles of the cooperative movement.

The *second* form of cooperative enterprise is that which

sells "for" its members. These co-ops are sometimes called producers' or workers' co-ops of which there are two main types. The first is a marketing co-op. Farmers, craftspeople and other independent business people can organize to retail their produce directly to the public, avoiding middlemen and sharing the savings or passing some on to the public. It should be noted that this form of cooperative organization is quite compatible with the free enterprise ethic since the individual producers are uninhibited in their private production sphere. Generally, a commercial and not a social accounting rationale guides the operations of marketing co-ops.

The other type of producer cooperative is fundamentally opposed to the free enterprise system. A true workers' co-op displaces the normal free enterprise arrangement of owner-employer and employee. Instead, the workers are owner, employer and employee. Management is drawn from the workers themselves and decisions are reached only after the full participation of all workers. However, unless the co-op is committed to other types of social aims, it remains a form of group capitalism, albeit on a democratic basis. Workers' cooperatives resemble collectives more than any other cooperative form.

The *third* form of cooperative enterprise is that which sells "to" its members. This form of cooperative is often called a consumers' co-op. These co-ops generally buy commodities, buildings, services and so forth at reduced prices and pass the savings on to co-op members. In most cases, these types of co-ops will have a commercial profit rationale, although there may also be social objectives.

The *fourth* form of cooperative enterprise is the cooperative credit union. In effect, it sells to and for its members. It takes the savings of its members and lends some of this money to its members. It is a way in which an association of people can raise and keep money within the community or association for whatever chosen purpose.

In conclusion, co-ops, like collectives, share with traditional businesses one similarity: business survival. If collectives and co-ops are unable to produce enough income to sustain their own members then the organizations disappear. But collectives and cooperatives differ from traditional businesses in that the former either distribute their surpluses (profits) according to the degree of member participation or apply the gains to meet certain social needs of the community.

The objectives of co-ops depend on the members' wishes.

What makes these groups different from big corporations is that with each member having one vote, the co-op must be more responsive to the collective will of its members. In a large corporation, a very tiny minority of shareholders can, and generally does, establish the objectives and the style of corporate management.

Community Organizations and Enterprises

When membership is broad, cooperatives and collectives can resemble community-owned activities. However, the latter are fundamentally different because they rely for some, if not all, of their revenue on public subscription, for example, individual, corporate and public grants, donations and membership fees. Community organizations and enterprises also have a large component of volunteer activity. Community organizations, when they sell their output, seldom charge full-cost prices for their goods or services. Generating self-sustaining operating revenues from sales, which is a harsh reality for co-ops and collectives, is generally a less important factor for community-owned enterprises and organizations. Consequently, community organizations are founded on and possess a strong social accounting rationale.

Because community organizations and enterprises are publicly owned, they are always controlled in varying degrees by the community and are accountable to it (through a board of directors) rather than to a limited private or collective ownership. What are typical community activities? At the local level, they are represented by community day-care centers, multi-purpose neighborhood community centers, services to the aged, storefront legal-aid clinics or amalgams of services produced by community development corporations. Some community organizations are less involved in direct service provision than in policy research, formulation and advocacy.

There is obviously a great diversity among community-owned organizations. To include them all under one heading and a single definition would be to render some of them an injustice. One type of community enterprise organization, particularly important from an economic standpoint but somewhat different from the rest, is the community development corporation. These community-owned corporations tend to be more involved in comprehensive local economic development--such as skill and employment development, community infrastructure development (schools, housing, clinics)--as well as in the provision of social services and needed goods.

Community development corporations are community-owned, dependent on a wide range of public support mechanisms, do not hesitate to use more traditional lines of credit for startup, often charge fair market rates for services rendered, and seek out delicate balances of economic (revenue raising) and social projects in order to remain self-supporting (that is, to secure continuous funding of a public and private nature).

A brief description of one particular group should help illustrate the nature of community development corporations. New Dawn is a community corporation founded in the early 1970s in Sydney, Nova Scotia.[3] As a result of continuous hard times in Cape Breton, a group of people sat down to ask what Cape Bretoners themselves could do to ease their economic plight. After establishing priority needs, the group sought the combination of public and private financing to begin to fulfill them. New Dawn became a type of holding company which eventually accumulated substantial assets. These allowed the company to perform socially useful and viable undertakings, as well as commercially profitable ones. As such, New Dawn became self-sustaining through a mix of public and private funding.

New Dawn has established dental clinics, low-cost housing, half-way houses, has operated senior citizens' homes and, in the process, created jobs and provided skill training. By 1980, New Dawn had injected $4 million into the Cape Breton area.[4] One participant has noted:

> New Dawn's purpose might be called primarily social: community improvement. However, the principal tool chosen to pursue this goal is business ... But is it possible, and even preferable, to answer the social needs of a community through groups of citizens organized in a more businesslike way?[5]

New Dawn's success to date would suggest an affirmative answer to this question.

Other general characteristics of community-owned organizations and enterprises can be dealt with briefly. The majority of them would be classed as "small business," having annual revenue of less than $2 million and fewer than 100 employees. Because most of these organizations are completely in the service sector, they tend to be very labor-intensive. The nature of many government funding programs reinforces this intensity by placing limits on the amount of capital equipment these organizations can purchase with grant money.

The output of community organizations is targeted very much towards social and economic improvement, environmental concerns, the development of amateur sport, recreation and athletic activities and arts and cultural pursuits. At the local level, the social "output" of community enterprises frequently consists of goods and services provided directly to clientele with special needs, usually without charge or at subsidized rates. Some community organizations may pursue a commercial profit, but not as an end in itself and only within a social accounting framework.

The "ownership" of these organizations is public. In some cases, a government department will virtually "own" an organization since it provides the major source of funding. In return, the organization may be required to fulfill specific functions, such as the provision of day-care services. In this case, the government is doing little more than contracting out a service which it feels responsible to provide. In the cases in which an organization is "widely held" because there are many public and private contributions, the organization can be deemed to be owned by its volunteer board of directors, drawn from the public and acting on the public's behalf.

The organization of the workplace varies according to the attitude and composition of the volunteer board, the chief executive's style and such things as the number of volunteers versus paid employees. Larger organizations often have hierarchical structures. Smaller community organizations are often very open, both to staff and volunteers, and decision making is consensual. Since the ownership of, and final responsibility for, community-based organizations is public and not private, at least the rationale is present to allow for more collective decision-making processes.

Voluntary Activity

Voluntary activity cannot be correctly defined as a distinct structure; it is more a form of activity especially structured to enable community organizations and enterprises to function. In fact, the majority of established community organizations (frequently called voluntary organizations) have been founded on voluntary effort, and their volunteer boards ultimately keep all community organizations accountable to the community at large.

In many smaller, and particularly emerging organizations, volunteers also do most of the fund raising, administrative and direct service work to ensure that the organization is strongly attached to the community. But as many organizations mature and grow, and perhaps become national in scope, the paid activity component (bureaucratization and professionalization) becomes more significant, while the volunteer board in some cases becomes the only direct contact with the community.

Barter and Skills Exchange

Barter and skills exchange are specialized forms of the mutual-aid village economy described below and in more detail in Appendix B. A novel form of bartering services is emerging known as "skills exchange." A skills exchange can operate on a very small scale or can become quite large and complex in an urban community. It consists of people providing a number of hours of skilled work to other members of the exchange in return for an equal number of hours of other's skilled work. Unlike unstructured neighborly cooperation in its simpler forms, however, a large urban skills exchange, aided by computers, can resemble the familiar monetized exchange activity of markets. Members need never know or meet many of the other members. As credits are built up in the exchange, they can be used to "purchase" other members' skills.

Barter, too, ranges from the simple exchange of goods among neighbors to intercorporate barter or even state-to-state barter. However, these latter activities are in no way informal merely because of the absence of a cash transaction.

Mutual Aid

This type of activity is found to some degree in small, rural and northern communities, in stable, older urban neighborhoods and in intentional cooperative communities. Mutual aid, a vital ingredient of community self-reliance, often stems from people trying to fulfill needs not addressed by the mainline, commercial economy. Not all, or much, trading or exchanging in these situations is done for profit or out of economic self-interest. The special social relationships engendered and permitted by these arrangements are primary for many people. The output of this type of economic activity is not preeminent as it is in the formal economy. Appendix B on the village economy describes in detail the workings of mutual aid.

City dwellers obviously do not have the same opportunities to be self-sufficient in food, fuel and housing that rural people do. As well, we associate mutual aid and neighborliness more with rural than urban life because in rural areas people know their neighbors better and depend on them more, and also because rural residents tend to have more of the all-round skills and tools needed to provide practical assistance to one another than does today's highly specialized urban population.

There is no doubt that urban households produce informally much less than rural ones. Nonetheless, in well-established and close knit urban neighborhoods, important elements of informal economic activity arise. For example, in immigrant neighborhoods with strong kinship networks, and in working class neighborhoods where residential turnover is low, there tends to be a significant level of mutual aid and exchange of unpaid labor with respect to child care, property maintenance and repair, and small community projects. While the informal production of goods may be quite limited, there is a significant informal production of services.

This network of informal economic exchange and mutual aid exists in neighborhoods in Toronto and Vancouver, as well as in Flin Flon, Manitoba, New Glasgow, Nova Scotia, Val d'Or, Quebec, and Nanaimo, British Columbia. There is no practical method of estimating the number of households for whom such activity is significant, much less for estimating the dollar value of this kind of activity. But its significance can be appreciated by considering the circumstances of those who can fall back on even this limited informal economy in difficult economic circumstances, in comparison with the circumstances of those who cannot. When jobs become scarce and wage and salary incomes fall, those with no family and community economic ties--people who are upwardly mobile, people who have moved to a strange part of the country for work or those involuntarily dislocated from their homes and communities--are more likely to be in serious financial trouble, and to be in it sooner than those who can fall back on family, neighborhood and community. These latter people may have a cushion which can sustain them through periods of difficulty without resort to bankruptcy, welfare, and the loss of assets, prestige and self-esteem. For example, it has been reported that many eastern Canadians, and especially Maritimers, who had moved to western Canada in the late 1970s in search of jobs and better pay, returned home when they became unemployed rather than stay on in the west.

A particular variant of the village economy is found in intentional communities: groups of people who by choice live and work together, often in a rural setting. Some of these communities may be dedicated to a particular belief, religious or otherwise, or to a central purpose, such as half-way homes. Most try to be as self-sufficient as possible, and to engage in mutual aid with similar communities or neighbors. They also seek to lead a holistic life, in opposition to the fragmentation and specialization they see in mainstream society. Their economic activity and organization are designed to produce an adequate level of basic goods and services, rather than abundance.

Household Activity

This activity likely represents the biggest single source of goods and services in the whole economy. Yet, it is probably the activity least recognized, valued and understood. However, economists have increasingly been turning their attention to household activity and recognizing its economic importance. *Home Inc.* and *After Industrial Society? The Emerging Self-Service Economy* are titles of some of the works in the mid-1970s that, bolstered by the feminist movement, have emphasized the significant economic contributions made by the household.[6]

The central reason household economic activity has gone largely unrecognized is that household "output" is not priced and exchanged. Consequently, it is difficult to estimate in quantitative terms. Additionally, one may ask, what is economic activity in the home? Cleaning dishes, repairing the washer, driving a child to a ball game, shaving, are these all economic activities? It could be claimed that the act of waking oneself up is an economic activity since hotels incur a financial cost performing this service for their guests.

Where do we draw the line between economic activity in the household and strictly social, personal and consumption activities related to daily living? At the outset, no definition is going to yield mutually exclusive categories. However, a definition of household production suggested in 1934 is as good as any in singling out those household activities which bear a relationship to activity carried out in the market sector and which we would generally refer to as economic. Household production:

> ... consists of those unpaid activities which are carried on, by and for the members, which activities might be replaced by market goods, or paid services, if circumstances such as income, market conditions, and personal inclinations permit the service being delegated to someone outside the household group.[7]

But even this definition can be ambiguous since it categorizes different activities as economic, depending on the particular household examined, the cultural context, the geographic region and the point in time. Some households would be less willing than others to contract out certain services, such as the care of elderly parents. In other words, for some households there are activities which form part of the family fabric or way of life and which would not, at certain times, be considered economic activities.

Moreover, some activities change over time in nature. Years ago, many males were shaved by professional barbers, but today most males would probably not consider shaving an economic activity. On the other hand, getting a home haircut is likely to be considered household economic activity. Brushing one's teeth daily could be done professionally by a dentist, but we know of no person who does this. Therefore, brushing one's teeth would not reasonably be classed as an economic activity.

The following concrete examples may be helpful to further our understanding of what would be considered economic activity: most housework, maintenance of house and equipment, food production and preparation, some child care and education, some home entertainment and recreation, much transportation and so on. In general, household economic activity mostly consists of activities that the majority of households in industrialized nations, to some extent and at various times, "contract out" to the market or public sectors.

Classifying Informal and Formal Structures

As noted in Chapter Three, there are various definitions of what informal activity encompasses. The definition attempted here encompasses most of the characteristics of previous descriptions but is more inclusive.

As a starting point, informal activity is that which is appropriate and democratic. And in order to achieve this, activity must be performed in small-scale structures that are guided by an operating rationale based on social (not private) accounting. Informal economic activity is that which solves the three basic problems of any economic system--what is produced, how it is produced and for whom it is produced--in a democratic manner which is appropriate to household and community needs.

This is opposed to formal economic activity which is often inappropriate or extraneous to household and community needs for three main reasons. Economic decisions in the private sector are guided by the need for private profit (which excludes a concern for social costs); effective economic demand is concentrated and not widely held (20 percent of the population controls over 40 percent of the purchasing power in almost all industrialized countries); and, lastly, decisions in the public sector are heavily biased in favor of the needs of a few politically powerful interests.

As Chapter Three underlined, admirers of informal economic activity emphasize certain characteristics that are either absent or diminished in formal activity. To recapitulate: informal activity is associated with more face-to-face contact, both among those making decisions and those affected by them; by more consensus-type decision making; by less specialization and stereo-typing; by fewer regulations; by more direct attention being paid to personal development; by more flexible work routines; by increased local decision making; by a greater reliance on personal and community resources; by the benefits of production being distributed more according to need; by the absence of capital accumulation for its own sake; by the reduced emphasis placed on money; by increased direct concern for the community, the environment and the welfare of future generations; and by more cooperation.

From this partial listing it can be seen that certain characteristics are chiefly associated with the scale of operation, while other characteristics are more closely associated with the rationale or objective of the economic activity. The fact that many formal economic structures are very large, for example, dictates certain characteristics contrary to those just enumer-ated--strong centralized decision making, hierarchical and author-itarian structures, written contracts, procedural manuals, anon-ymity, limited face-to-face contact between staff and manage-

ment, impersonal and formal working relationships, little interaction between owners/managers and consumers, headquarters and
plants physically separated by great distances and so forth.
Economic activity carried out in small units, however, tends to
exhibit the opposite characteristics.

But the operating rationale, reflecting the basic objective of
economic activity, in itself also strongly influences the character
of the activity. Whether a unit's activities are based on a
commercial or social accounting rationale largely determines, in
conjunction with size, the manner in which the basic economic
questions of what, how, for whom and why goods and services are
produced. Being guided primarily by commercial profit and other
economic indicators, rather than consideration of the full and
ultimate consequences of economic activity on the individual,
household and community (referred to as social accounting), lends
certain unique characteristics to economic activity. For example,
in the formal economy the individual worker is often reduced to
a "factor of production," to use a traditional economic term. The
decision to use either a piece of machinery or a person to perform
a task is devoid of human considerations. The answer depends on
which factor of production can perform the function more cheaply
and efficiently from the standpoint of being appropriate to private
profit considerations. In the formal economy, land, labor and
capital are anonymously lumped together. Labor is spouseless,
childless and without neighbors and community. It is primarily a
factor to be manipulated for commercial profit and constrained
only by law, the market and trade unions.

A commercial profit rationale also provides a style for
determining what is produced and for whom. Consumers with the
most money have wider influence over the types and quantities of
goods and services produced. Need is irrelevant. Contrast this to
the well-functioning household in the informal economy. It is
hard to imagine a parent apportioning dinner among the children
according to the highest bidder and designing the menu according
to dollar votes; here, direct concern for human and social
considerations outranks the commercial.

As helpful as this above listing of characteristics is, it does
not provide a useful definition of informal. But if scale of
operation and accounting rationale are good proxies for indicating
formal and informal activity, these two factors can be identified.
Figure 3 below illustrates how units of economic activity can be
classified according to scale and rationale. On the horizontal axis
is located the operating rationale, extending from extremely

commercial to extremely social--with gradations in between. On the vertical axis is located the scale of operation, with the small-scale extreme being represented by a single-person productive activity and the large-scale extreme represented by the large corporation or centralized public bureaucracies.

FIGURE 3

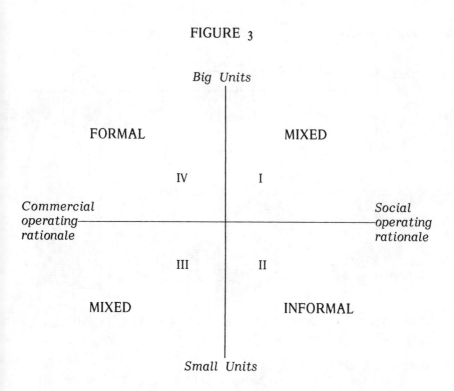

We would then allocate all economic structures in the whole economy, according to the configuration of economic units shown in Figure 4. Admittedly, there are "grey" areas where our definition is less useful. But in general, classifying economic activity by scale and operating rationale is a step forward in trying to operationalize the definition of informal. If economic data were collected according to the nine sectors outlined in the whole economy spectrum, it would be possible to develop measures that would tell us the extent of shifts between informal and formal economic activity.

FIGURE 4

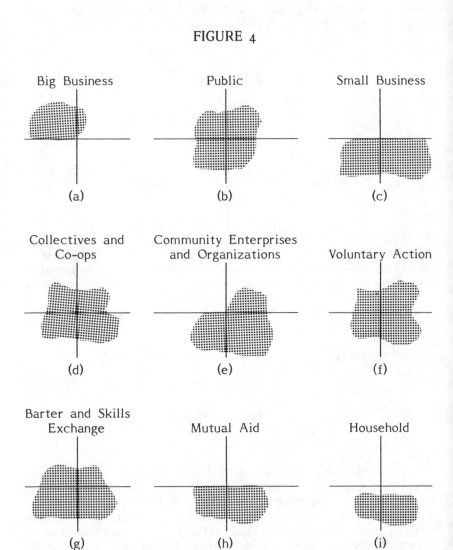

Big Business

(a)

Public

(b)

Small Business

(c)

Collectives and Co-ops

(d)

Community Enterprises and Organizations

(e)

Voluntary Action

(f)

Barter and Skills Exchange

(g)

Mutual Aid

(h)

Household

(i)

CHAPTER FIVE

MEASURING INFORMAL ECONOMIC ACTIVITY

This chapter attempts two tasks: to give an impression of the volume of activity and output in the informal economy and to indicate the extent to which these activities and outputs are excluded from conventional GNP accounting. Because the activities of the big business and public sectors are well recorded they are not dealt with here.

Various size indicators can be used in attempting to measure the informal economy. These include: number of participants; number of establishments, organizations or work units; amount of time devoted to the activity; and value of investment and output. As already noted, the preeminent measure of formal economic activity is total value of current output (GNP). The reason informal activity tends to be omitted from GNP is that much of its output does not enter the marketplace and consequently has no recorded market price. To some extent, this problem can be overcome by imputing a market equivalent value--or shadow price--to these outputs. Attempts by economists and others to do this are reviewed, and we discuss the major inherent limitations of assigning dollar values to informal activity. As incomplete and inadequate as the data are, this summary is presented in order to show that substantial time is devoted to informal economic activity, even if we do not care to ascribe a dollar value to it.

Small Business Enterprises

Only recently has the federal government begun collecting data on small-scale businesses. A small business is defined as a business that has annual sales of less than $2 million. This level of sale typically corresponds to between 15 and 100 employees per firm depending on the sector, for example, manufacturing, construction, trade and service. The following statistics give some idea of the relative size of the small business sector. (Self-employed businesses are excluded from the definition but are discussed later.)

In 1978, the latest year studied, there were 724,000 businesses in Canada--97 percent of these were small businesses with sales of less than $2 million annually, 85 percent had sales of less than $250,000 and 48 percent were very small with sales of less than $50,000 annually.[1]

In terms of total economic value contributed by business to GNP, the small business sector's share was 29 percent--equal to $25 billion in 1978. In contrast, the very largest businesses (sales exceeding $20 million) were the source of 48 percent of business GNP. Very small businesses (annual sales less than $250,000) contributed a 10 percent share--close to $9 billion worth of goods and services.

Some 2.7 million people were employed in the small business sector in 1978, representing 42 percent of all business employees in Canada. The smallest businesses (sales less than $50,000) employed 6 percent of the total. The average number of employees in all businesses in Canada was twelve, not a very "typical" figure since the smallest firms employed only one person, while the largest employed over 1,000 persons. In the small business sector as a whole, the average figure per business was four employees.

Not surprisingly, a greater share of small businesses are Canadian-controlled, although the data do not show whether Canadian control also means local control. Nonetheless, while large businesses (sales over $2 million) constitute only 3 percent of all businesses in Canada, they do account for two-thirds of all foreign-controlled businesses. About one in five large firms is foreign-controlled, but less than 1 percent of small businesses are controlled from abroad.

As noted, small business statistics exclude the self-employed. There are about one-half million self-employed in Canada. Farmers constitute the largest group of self-employed, followed by professionals, commissioned salesmen and fishermen. But the self-employed group is growing (6 percent annually) and since 1973 (excluding farmers) its rate of growth of employment has been more than double that of paid employees.

Cooperatives and Collectives

Data on cooperatives and collectives are difficult to come by. Statistics Canada has collected data on cooperative manufacturing operations, but because the manufacturing sector only employs about 20 percent of the labor force its coverage is very limited.[2] For 1978 their data show that of the 32,000 manufacturing establishments in Canada, 197 or 1 percent were cooperatives employing 17,000 people. Of these 197 cooperatives, 40 percent were in Quebec. As a share of all manufacturing businesses within a province, however, Saskatchewan at 4 percent led by a considerable margin. Manufacturing cooperatives seem to be on the decline when measured by their share of all manufacturing businesses: 3.1 percent in 1950, 2.5 percent in 1960, 1.6 percent in 1970 and 1 percent in 1978.

Another source of data on cooperatives is the annual review published by the Co-operative Union of Canada.[3] Summary data for operating year 1980-1981 are given in Table 1 on page 76.

In addition to these numbers, there is a housing co-op sector involving 877 incorporated co-ops with 20,500 units built, 5,729 under construction or renovation and 5,800 in the planning stage. All numbers in this report are conservative because co-ops not affiliated with large federations are generally excluded. Many small retail co-op operations fall into this category, as do most small worker co-ops and collectives. The Co-operative Union estimates these small emerging co-ops are increasing at an annual rate of 30 percent.

Community Enterprises and Organizations

The closest estimate of the amount of activity in this sector comes from statistics on "charitable organizations" registered with the federal government. Since registration as a charitable organization permits tax-deductible public donations, it is worthwhile for most not-for-profit organizations to register, but not all do. The information collected in this manner thus gives a conservative estimate of the amount of activity. Some organizations choose not to register, some have not yet registered and others (especially economic enterprises) are not always eligible, even though they are incorporated as non-profit corporations.

TABLE I

Summary Data on Cooperatives, 1980-1981

Type of Co-op	Employees	Members	Sales ($MM)	Assets ($MM)
Local Retail, Supply	26,603	1,073,206	3,705	1,973
Grain Handling	9,461	226,691	5,032	1,962
Trust, Insurance Credit Unions	9,538*	17,140,000**	--	40,520
Fishery Co-ops	2,641	7,705	175	112
Dairy Co-ops	7,321	33,362	1,428	437
Totals	55,519	18,480,964	10,340	45,004

*Employee numbers for credit unions were estimated on the basis of known asset/employee ratios for co-op trusts.

**Excludes co-op trusts. About 9.8 million persons hold accounts in credit unions and 7.4 million persons are policy holders with insurance co-ops. Undoubtedly, there is much overlapping of members across the two groups.

In 1980, there were 39,965 registered charities in Canada, not including community hospitals and teaching institutions.[4] Of these registered charities 24,026 were religious institutions, most of which, in addition to providing their traditional spiritual functions, were involved in community, social service and economic activities.

The charitable sector had revenues of $5.8 billion in 1980, in comparative terms equal to 11 percent of all federal government revenues. Although the number of paid employees in this sector is not known, one estimate has placed it at around 175,000 employees[5] or 4.3 employees per community organization. The estimated GNP contribution generated by these paid employees (volunteer contributions are dealt with below) was $2.5 billion in 1980.

Volunteer Activity

Most organized volunteer activity is devoted to community enterprises (politically related activities are not considered here as community enterprise). Thanks to a 1979-1980 Statistics Canada survey, we now have an estimate of organized volunteer activity in Canada: 2.7 million Canadians volunteered 374 million hours in a 12-month period in 1979-1980, equaling about 200,000 person-years of work.[6]

When artificially converted into dollar figures, volunteer work contributed an estimated $2 billion to GNP in 1979-1980.[7] The combined contribution of registered charities and volunteers would have equaled $4.5 billion or 1.7 percent of GNP in 1980.

Barter and Skills Exchange

Legally, all barter (and probably skills exchange) should be registered with Revenue Canada. Certainly, all barter and exchange involving the producer's primary occupation are subject to tax treatment. But undoubtedly, except for commercial establishments, very few if any of these informal exchanges are recorded anywhere either by Revenue Canada or in Statistics Canada surveys.

Consequently, there are very few data on barter and skills exchange. At the same time, most people are aware of some barter or skills exchange in their community. Moreover, in the past decade, it is strongly apparent that these forms of economic activity are growing.

We know of at least two successfully organized skills exchanges in British Columbia on Vancouver Island. Until a survey is done, it is impossible to assess the amount of barter and skills exchange among Canadians.

Mutual Aid in Northern
and Rural Economies

The value of economic output derived from mutual aid in many small communities is substantially underrated. The main reason is that since much of this output is for local consumption and is not exchanged in the marketplace, no price is ascribed to it and it is thus excluded from GNP.

The best way to get some idea of the volume of domestic economic activity is to look at some documented examples of it in various locations to see if any generalizations can be made. There are numerous studies of small and remote village economies by anthropologists, sociologists and geographers (and, as it happens, almost none by economists). The following discussion is drawn from this research.

Table 2 on the opposite page compares the results of recent studies (1970 to 1983) of country food production (i.e., fish, game and plants) in a variety of Indian and Inuit communities across northern Canada. Government agencies either do not record this production at all or they drastically underestimate it. For example, in the Mackenzie Valley and Western Arctic during the early 1970s, the actual production of country food was estimated annually at 2.2 million kilograms, compared to officially recorded totals of only .8 million kilograms.[9]

While the data in Table 2 are neither uniformly reliable nor directly comparable, they do indicate a consistent pattern over very large areas of the Canadian North, and typify the situation for tens of thousands of people there. Per capita meat and fish consumption by Canadians as a whole, by comparison, has ranged from about 80 to 120 kilograms over the same period: this is lower, and sometimes much lower, than in northern communities.

Almost none of this food is sold for cash, and hence we cannot determine its value on the basis of market price. Nonetheless, we can estimate, using a replacement cost approach, what northern households would have to pay for this quantity and quality of food if they did not produce it for themselves. However, we have the problem of identifying the appropriate substitute: what is the locally acceptable replacement for moose or caribou, if indeed one can be found? Using domestic red meats, fowl and similar fish species as substitutes for country food, and by making adjustments for differing protein content, it has been found that effective replacement values for country food now range from $5 to $20 per kilogram in isolated northern communities. Country food production thus contributes hundreds, or more usually thousands, of dollars annually to per capita income.[10]

TABLE 2

Annual Per Capita Country Food Production in Selected Northern Native Communities or Regions

Region or Community	Edible Weight (kgs.)
Northern Labrador (Inuit)	131
Northern Quebec (Inuit)	c.439
James Bay, Quebec (Cree)	c.139
Northeastern Saskatchewan (Cree)	532
Northeastern B.C. (Beaver)	c.220
Ross River, Yukon (Kaska)	284
Mackenzie Valley & Beaufort Sea (Dene and Inuit)	109
Baker Lake, N.W.T. (Inuit)	320
Pond Inlet, N.W.T. (Inuit)	204

Sources: See Notes at end of text (Chapter Five, reference number 8).

This amount does not include the imputed value of domestically produced firewood, clothing and bedding, all derived from the produce of the land. On the other hand, we have not deducted the cost of production of all of these goods from their gross values. No matter how it is calculated, however, the value of domestic production remains striking in comparison with Native peoples' cash income in small communities.

When the value of this domestic income is ignored, as is so often the case in economic accounts, hunting, fishing and trapping communities are commonly seen to be poverty stricken, with income derived mostly from commodity sales and transfer payments in inadequate amounts. Hence, there is obviously a desperate need for wage labor. The inclusion of domestic income radically alters this view. In the early 1970s, for example, it was calculated for the western Northwest Territories that income from fur, fish and game provided about 50 percent of Native income, with game being by far the most important contributor.[11] In 1979 in northern Labrador, traditional production accounted for 25 percent of total personal income, transfer payments for 34 percent and wage employment for 41 percent (with employment in the fish plants generated by local resource production accounting for a significant part of that figure).[12] This was in contrast to the national situation in which nearly 80 percent of personal income is derived from wages, about 8 percent from transfer payments and, according to the data-gathering system in current use in Canada, virtually none from production analogous to that in the Native economy.[13]

Numerous studies undertaken in Newfoundland in the 1960s showed that the domestic production of food and firewood in the outports amounted to 13 to 18 percent of per household income.[14] When the value of owner-built housing was added, domestic production accounted for as much as 47 percent per household. Data from the 1970s suggest that these figures have by no means declined.

About 80 percent of rural houses in Newfoundland are owner-built. As a consequence, 84 percent of owner-occupied, non-farm buildings in Newfoundland are mortgage free, compared to 44 percent in Ontario. (The respective figures for Newfoundland and Ontario in urban areas are 72 and 40 percent, and in rural areas, 92 and 58 percent.) In 1971, it was estimated that 20 percent of lumber consumption in Newfoundland was accounted for by home-produced lumber which never entered the marketplace, and production has probably not declined since. It has been recently estimated that throughout Newfoundland, including urban centers like St. John's, about 43 percent of households burn wood. This figure is thought to be increasing, although as some of this wood is cut and sold commercially it cannot all be attributed to domestic production.

Many of these evaluations of the village or informal economies of Newfoundland and the North were undertaken in response to attempts to industrialize and formalize their economies. In Newfoundland, the outports were being closed down, and work or leisure does not hold up very strongly. Among employed males, for example, after deducting 10.4 daily hours for personal care (mainly sleep), of the remaining 13.6 hours, 50 percent is devoted to regular paid work, 34 percent to leisure and 16 percent to informal work activity.

TABLE 3

Daily Time Budget, Halifax 1971
(in Hours)

Activity	Males		Females	
	Employed	Non-Employed	Employed	Non-Employed
Regular Paid Work and Related	6.8	0.4	5.3	0.6
Voluntary	0.1	0.2	0.1	0.6
Housework	0.7	1.3	2.3	4.4
Marketing	0.3	0.3	0.4	0.4
Child Care	0.5	0.7	0.6	1.5
Personal Care (eating, sleeping, health, etc.)	10.4	12.0	11.0	11.3
Study	0.3	2.1	0.1	0.1
Leisure (recreation, social, entertainment, travel, etc.)	4.4	6.6	4.4	5.1
Total*	24.0	24.0	24.0	24.0

*Due to rounding, columns may not precisely add to 24 hours.

Source: Adapted from D.H. Elliott, A.S. Harvey and D. Procos, "An Overview of the Halifax Time-Budget Study," Institute of Public Affairs, Dalhousie University, October 1973, p. 16.

reduction in household size is not only due to more people living alone. The average family size has also fallen from 4.2 persons in 1931 to 3.3 in 1981. The share of multi-family households has also declined. In 1951, two or more families sharing a household comprised 6.7 percent of all households, but by 1971 this number has been reduced to 2 percent.

From the standpoint of the study of the household as an economic unit, these trends cannot fail to alter the traditional way households have allocated their time and resources between formal and informal economic activities, as well as the patterns of sharing the rewards from these various activities. The significant decline in the number of household members, the increase in single-person households and the rise in the number of multi-earner households all suggest that the amount of time and the number of complementary household workers available to each household for household activity has fallen over the years.

Time-Use Studies

One method for ascertaining what activities households pursue and the time allocated to them is to examine time-use data. Examination of these data does not directly reveal the value of household output, but rather how households allocate their time between formal and informal economic activities. Time-use information thus provides the first necessary building block for constructing estimates of the value of household activity.

In Canada, there is little detailed information available on time-use. Table 3 on page 84 presents the results of one well-known study.[19] It shows that women, employed or without paid employment, do most household-related work (housework, child care, marketing). Household work performed by women without paid employment amounts to 6.3 hours per day, more time than employed women spend at their jobs and almost as much time as employed men spend at theirs. But employed women spend 1.7 hours more than women without paid employment on a combination of paid work, housework, marketing and child care. Males with paid work spend 5.6 hours more than their counterparts without paid employment on this same combination of work. Employed women would seem to have the longest work day of all groups.

Interestingly, and although much favored in mainstream economic analysis, the conventional division of time between paid

For employed females, the traditional dichotomy is even more strained with the respective shares being 40 percent regular work, 33 percent leisure and 27 percent informal activity. Consequently, what one does in their non-regular work time is not necessarily leisure but often some other form of work activity without pay.

Time allocated to informal work activities is most pronounced among women who are not employed. The breakdown of their day (after deducting personal care hours) is 53 percent work, 42 percent leisure and 5 percent regular work (or simply "work" in the traditional economic classification). When work is defined as only paid work, such as employment (now the standard definition), the traditional dichotomy of time between work and leisure has no meaning whatsoever to the homemaker.

The trading off (not necessarily voluntarily) of time between paid work and non-paid work activity is clearly demonstrated in the case of males not employed. In comparison to the employed, of the 6.4 daily hours less that the unemployed do not devote to regular paid work, 2.7 of these hours are devoted to increased informal work activity.

As interesting as these finds are, however, they represent only one large study done for a limited time only during 1971. But studies from other countries and conducted for other time periods show the same general results, and further illustrate how a household allocates time among activities as well as among household members.

Table 4 on the next page presents some results from a U.S. study of the time-use of 1,400 households conducted in the late 1960s.[20] This study found that the amount of time homemakers spend on household work depends heavily on two variables: number and age of children, with younger children requiring more time, and outside employment of the homemaker.

Besides the results shown in the table, the authors uncovered the following factors: the work week for employed wives varies from 66 to 75 hours (the coming leisure society?); the husband's average weekly household work contribution does not increase if his wife takes outside employment; and each teenager contributes one hour daily towards household work, while younger children (6-11 years) contribute one-half hour each.

Finally, as also noted in the Halifax study (Table 3), in spite of the long hours devoted to all forms of work by employed wives and mothers, outside employment does call for a reduction or a trade-off in informal (household) activity. The time devoted to

TABLE 4

Average Hours Per Day Spent on Various Household Activities by Homemakers and by All Workers in United States, 1967-1968

| Households | | Food-related Activities | | House Care | | Care of Clothing | | Family Care | | Marketing and Management | | All Household Work | | All Work* |
Kinds	Number	Home-makers	All Workers	Home-makers	All Workers	Home-makers	All Workers	Home-makers	All Workers	Home-makers	All Workers	Home-makers	All Workers	Home-makers
No Children:														
Non-employed homemaker	97	2.0	2.3	1.5	2.2	1.1	1.2	0.1	0.2	0.9	1.4	5.7	7.2	6.6
Employed homemaker	71	1.3	1.5	0.9	1.4	0.6	0.7	0.1	0.3	0.8	1.2	3.7	5.0	9.4
1 Child:														
Non-employed homemaker	149	2.1	2.3	1.5	2.3	1.1	1.2	1.8	2.4	1.0	1.5	7.4	9.7	8.0
Employed homemaker	61	1.6	2.0	1.3	2.0	0.8	0.9	0.7	1.5	0.7	1.3	5.1	7.7	9.6
4-6 Children:														
Non-employed homemaker	186	2.4	3.1	1.7	3.1	1.4	1.6	2.2	3.2	1.0	1.9	8.7	12.8	9.3
Employed homemaker	39	1.9	3.1	1.2	2.8	1.2	1.5	1.1	2.2	0.9	1.8	6.3	11.3	10.3

*Includes small amounts of part-time outside employment for the non-employed homemaker.

Source: Kathryn Walker, "Household Work Time: Its Implication for Family Decisions," *Journal of Home Economics* 65, no. 7 (October 1973), pp. 10-11. Reprinted by permission.

outside employment is not drawn entirely from leisure hours. Yet, conventional economic wisdom and national accounting procedures would have us believe that the contribution household members make to the formal economy is not offset by a reduction in informal output elsewhere. Time-use results show otherwise.

In 1975, American households performed a good deal of household repairs and maintenance of cars and consumer durables. Table 5 on the following page presents the results of a national survey involving more than 1,000 households.[21] The results indicate that much of the work performed in the household closely parallels the work performed in the formal (market) economy.

Household work is not all washing-up, cleaning floors, shopping and caring for children. These activities we perhaps normally think of as having weak market (economic) associations and, therefore, we discount them as economic activities. But it becomes more difficult to justify the exclusion of activities such as painting, plumbing, carpentry and car and TV repair from any accounting of a nation's total economic activity. Yet, Table 5 shows that over two-thirds of all household painting, papering and carpentry work, and over one-half of all household plumbing, electrical and masonry work, are performed "free" by the household members themselves. And on average, almost one-third of the households reported various types of work being performed on their households, cars and appliances in 1975 by household members.

Do households today allocate their members' time differently than in earlier years? As interesting as the answer would be, the absence of reliable and comparable earlier studies makes an investigation difficult without relying heavily on anecdotal material.[22] Nonetheless, a few authors have attempted to make comparisons, using the most relevant and comparable data available.

Comparing pre-1965 studies to the results of the 1965-1975 American national surveys, John Robinson concludes that there is no evidence of increasing free or leisure time among adults.[23] He further finds that while there was a reduction of routine housework activity, there was more time being spent on the managerial aspects of housekeeping, as well as child rearing and shopping. (Perhaps shopping is becoming an American leisure activity?)

However, comparing the 1965 and 1975 American national time-use survey results, Robinson concludes: employed men and women spent less time at their jobs; time spent on family care

TABLE 5

Percent of Households Reporting Repairs
or Maintenance of Homes, Cars and Appliances
in United States, 1975

Type of Repair	Percent of All Households Reporting Repair Being Done	Of the Households Reporting Repairs Being Done:		
		Percent Paying Someone to Do Repair	Percent Doing Repair Themselves	Percent Both Paying Someone to Do Repair and Doing Repair Themselves
Inside Painting	43.2	16.5	85.3	1.8
Outside Painting	26.7	28.7	73.3	2.0
Papering	16.1	20.1	81.6	1.7
Plumbing	41.1	50.7	52.1	2.8
Electrical	23.1	43.3	59.1	2.4
Carpentry	20.1	32.6	68.9	1.5
Masonry	7.8	42.0	59.4	1.4
TV Repair	34.4	87.4	14.2	1.6
Other Household Appliances	21.5	66.5	34.0	0.5
Car Repair	65.1	76.3	32.3	8.6

Source: Reprinted by permission of the author and publisher from Martha F. Hill, "Investments of Time in Houses and Durables," Chapter 9 in Thomas E. Juster and Frank P. Stafford, eds., *Time, Goods and Well-Being* (Ann Arbor: Institute for Social Research, University of Michigan, Fall 1985).

(routine housecleaning, meal preparation, etc.) dropped 20 percent; all women devoted less time to work, while men increased their work time; and free time increased by 10 percent. How this free time was used altered considerably. More time was spent watching TV, pursuing adult education and recreational activity, while less time was devoted to visiting and other informal social activities.

Joann Vanek's study of time-use over an approximately 50-year period in the U.S. yields results similar to Robinson's for earlier periods. Her study gives a broad breakdown by household activity.[24] She concludes that for full-time homemakers the time spent on household work was the same in 1965 as it was in the 1920s--55 hours per week.

The major activity has always been food preparation (20 hours), followed by home care (12 hours). Clothing care, shopping, managerial tasks and family care consume about 8 hours each. But while the total weekly number of hours remain the same, the composition has changed. Although less time is spent today on food preparation, more time is devoted to family care and to shopping and managerial tasks. There has been little change in housecleaning time. Curiously enough, the amount of time spent on laundry has increased. Presumably, this is due to the fact that people have more clothes now, wash them more often and send out less laundry.

In comparison with women employed outside their homes, contemporary non-employed homemakers spend twice as many hours (55 versus 26 hours weekly) at housework. But because many more women are employed outside their homes today, the amount of housework performed by contemporary U.S. women is much less today than 50 years earlier. Vanek also observes that husbands of employed women lend no more housework assistance than do the husbands of non-employed women, and the amount in either case is very small, limited primarily to shopping. Consequently, the total amount of time spent on household production has surely declined over the 50 years under study.

A trend over the period 1961-1974 in the U.K. tends to verify some of the conclusions reached by Robinson for the period 1965-1975 in the U.S. These results vary with the trends noted for earlier periods.[25] The U.K. study concluded there has been about a 5-18 percent increase in leisure time, depending on employment status (the retired having the smallest gain in leisure); a substantial transfer of women's work from the household into the formal economy; a limited transfer of household work from women to men (about 10 percent); and an increase of non-passive leisure activities outside the home, such as sports, parties, dances and visiting friends.

Work: For Love or Money--The Conceptual Difficulties in Assigning Dollar Values to Informal Output

Attempting to estimate household production through time-use studies is one method of showing the enormous amount of time devoted to this type of economic activity. Some researchers, however, go further by taking these time-use data and converting them into dollar values. When they do this, however, they not only demonstrate the operational difficulties in doing so but also the inappropriateness of placing a dollar value on informal activity.

At the base of this conversion attempt is the definition of household production which is essentially that adopted in Chapter Four. People attempting to estimate the value of household production must first designate those activities which are done by and for the household and could, if desirable and financially possible, be purchased in the marketplace. As a theoretical construct, this definition is quite useful since it awakens us to a wide range of household activity which is, in fact, "economic"--for example, food production, home repair and the like. But to go beyond this concept and single out specific activities with dollar values is something else.

Virtually everything that goes on within a household can be purchased in the market. Caring, affection, companionship and people who will relieve your loneliness are all available for hire--just consult the yellow pages. And when these services are provided by the marketplace, they are classed as economic and their value enters GNP (if they are legal and declared). But surely, when these caring and comforting functions take place in the home, they are not economic. And this represents the whole problem in trying to value, in dollar terms, most of the activities and functions performed in the household and among friends and neighbors.[26]

Oranges, cars and washing machines can properly be enumerated in dollar terms because they are produced to be exchanged anonymously with consumers. In fact, who consumes the output is irrelevant to the producer. But the comfort, affection and learning which accompany many activities performed in the home cannot be enumerated in dollar terms as if they could be exchanged for a pair of pants or a bottle of whiskey. To place a dollar value on the output of all human activity is to assume that all of these varied outputs are commodities interchangeable within some great comprehensive market of goods and services. It assumes that one hour of a parents' caring for a child, artificially valued at $10 per hour, is exchangeable for 10 dozen oranges at $1 per dozen.

A human has many needs, not all of which can be evaluated in dollar terms. Some things simply cannot be substituted by other items in the market basket simply because they are deemed to be of equivalent dollar value. Many services performed in the home are often quite correctly described as "priceless," which is why all attempts to measure the dollar value of household economic activity are bound to have shortcomings. These represent attempts to take purposefully developed activities outside the market sector and recast them as market goods and services produced anonymously and at lowest cost.

Nonetheless, people insist on knowing the "ball-park" estimates of household economic activity. To be sure, much household production can be at least partially cast in dollar terms. Certainly, some household production for some people is a conscious trade-off with outputs produced by the exchange economy. And certainly, when prices rise faster than wages, households will seek to substitute household production for market production.

After selecting "economic" household activities, it becomes necessary to place a dollar value on them. This is difficult because value in the marketplace is determined by exchange. There are suppliers (producers) and demanders (consumers) whose interaction determines price (economic value). Indeed, because household production does not include exchange among its members for money, it is extremely difficult to construct market price estimates for these different outputs if they were traded in the market. Consequently, investigators have developed different estimating techniques.[27]

The two most common methods of valuing household activity concentrate entirely on the supply or cost side by estimating the value of the labor input. Hence, they ignore the demand or consumer side. The two methods are known as replacement cost and opportunity cost. In the replacement cost approach, each household activity is assigned a time value. The time devoted to an activity is valued at the rate a professional would have charged in the market. Thus, a homemaker becomes a composite of a chef, chauffeur, medical attendant, launderer and so on. There are several shortcomings to this approach.

First, professionals may well take less time to perform a given task since their productivity is higher. Therefore, this method may overvalue household activity. Secondly, if professional market rates were charged in the household, it might forego certain activities or reduce its consumption of them. If a homemaker charged chef rates, then more household members would make their own meals, or perhaps even eat out more often. Thirdly, the value of other inputs contributed by household members is ignored. Garden food, the use of tools for repair and the like all add to the value of straight labor time. Fourthly, there may be qualitative differences. Perhaps the quality of some professional work is higher. But also in many cases (especially involving human service activities), perhaps the quality of service provided by household members is higher. The replacement cost approach makes no adjustment for quality or any of the above factors.

The second method is known as the opportunity cost approach. This method stems from a strong economic tradition of valuing goods, services and labor time, not by what they are worth in the market but what could have been produced or performed instead--that is, what were the best foregone opportunities or alternatives. This opportunity "cost" then is interpreted as being the value of producing the good or service in question or as being the real value of the time spent. When this method is used to value the goods and services produced by the homemaker, it does not do precisely that. Rather, it simply values the presumed opportunity cost of the homemaker's time.

The major shortcoming of this approach is that all activity performed by the homemaker is presumed to have equal economic value per time unit. Whether the homemaker is washing dishes, repairing the car or educating the children, all are valued at the wage which the homemaker could be receiving in the market, i.e., the financial opportunities foregone. And this leads to another serious shortcoming. If two homemakers perform household activities at the same efficiency and of the same quality, but one is a neurosurgeon and the other a floor cleaner in their market employments, then the household output of the neurosurgeon will be credited as being about ten times more valuable than the identical output of the floor cleaner. This is obviously a very biased and faulty technique for estimating the true economic value of household output.

Both the replacement cost and opportunity cost techniques ignore the demand side of the valuation operation. The economic value of a good or service not only depends on the labor and other costs of producing it but on the evaluation of the good or service by the consumer. The implications of this for the value of household production are enormous. All goods and services produced are not of equal quality. An hour of child care is not identical in all households. We would have to question the consumers--in this case, the children--to find out what value they place on home child care.

If homemakers perform their activities in a manner that upsets other household members and leads to discomfort, these should not be valued at the same level as identical activities performed by homemakers who are able to make their households pleasant and comfortable. Unfortunately, because the replacement and opportunity cost methods ignore the valuations of the goods and services produced by household members, all household activities anywhere are assumed to be qualitatively identical. These methods lead to faulty estimations of output in the household sector. The question of appropriateness of using dollar valuation methods for many of the activities performed within the household is again raised.

There is a third, but less popular, method of estimating the value of household activities where there is a clear market equivalent. This is the value-added approach. It has been used to estimate the value of home, appliance and car repair by asking each household how much it saved by doing the repair work itself. Each household estimates what the market equivalent cost would have been, then subtracts the cost of the tools and materials it purchased to perform the repair. The difference is the value added by the household which becomes the value of the household activity. While this method combines both supply and demand elements, it requires more data and survey work and is somewhat subjective.

Based on one or the other of these estimating procedures, what do the empirical studies tend to show with respect to the value of household activity? Keeping in mind all of the shortcomings of estimating household output, and recognizing that the results are strictly "ball-park" estimates, most studies conclude that household output in Canada and the U.S. is equivalent to 40 percent of GNP. This would mean that Canada's 1985 GNP, adjusted for household production, would be about $630 billion rather than around $450 billion.

A study performed for Statistics Canada by H.J. Adler and O. Hawrylsyshyn for the years 1961 and 1971, using both the opportunity and replacement cost methods, concluded that household activity in 1961 was between 40-44 percent of GNP, and in 1971 between 40-41 percent.[28] Unfortunately, the researchers used 1971 time-use data for both years so the trend estimate is of limited value. Of the total output of households, about two-thirds was contributed by females. Proulx, using the replacement cost method, estimated that for Canada in 1971 the value of household output equaled between 35 to 40 percent of GNP.[29]

For the U.S., a replacement cost study by W. Gauger and K. Walker based on 1967 data concluded that household output for husband-wife families only was equivalent to 26 percent of GNP, and 75 percent of this output was attributable to women.[30] Since husband-wife families represented only 56 percent of all households at that time, it is reasonable to expect that the value of total household output would be in the neighborhood of 40 percent of GNP.

Finally, Martha Hill, in her study of home, car and appliance repair, estimates that U.S. households produced the equivalent of $30 billion worth of output on these projects alone in 1975.[31] Using the value-added approach, she calculated that each household contributed about $442. (In 1985's inflated dollars this is equivalent to about $930.)

Additionally, Carter Henderson has reported that during 1977, 43 percent of the U.S. non-farm households produced the equivalent of $14 billion worth of fruits and vegetables, primarily for private consumption.[32] This is equal to about $200 per household which in 1985 dollars would represent about $360.

Physical Assets

Another indicator of the size of household production is the value and extent of physical assets--that is, assets which are capable of producing goods and services within the household and which, in the business sector, would be referred to as capital investment. Because we are not in the habit of viewing the household as a producing unit we tend to overlook the fact that much of a household's expenditure is, like business expenditure, devoted to durables which are, in turn, used to produce further goods and services. Yet, we label these purchases "consumer" durables when made by the household and "producer" durables when bought by businesses. In fact, they are producer durables for both.

What is the extent of physical assets owned by Canadian households? In 1980, almost two-thirds of Canadian households owned their own homes, and almost one-half of these were owned clear of mortgage.[33] In rural areas, almost 90 percent of homes are owned and 60 percent are mortgage free. This latter fact illustrates to some extent the greater degree of mutual aid and self-reliance among rural households. Over three-quarters of Canadian households have electric washing machines, two-thirds have clothes dryers, 29 percent have dishwashers, 51 percent have freezers (75 percent in rural areas), 97 percent have television sets, over one-quarter have overnight camping equipment and 80 percent have at least one automobile. Thus, just this partial list demonstrates that Canadian households are extensively equipped to produce a considerable amount of goods and services.

It is difficult to estimate the total worth of these household producer durables, but it is known how much households spend per year adding to the stock of these durables. This can be compared with the amount that business spends on investment. If contruction--both residential and commercial--is excluded, the household invested $26.4 billion in durables, and the business sector (including public business enterprises) invested $28.7 billion in machinery and equipment in 1981.[34] Consequently, the household and business sectors are adding to their capital stocks (less buildings) at almost the same rate today, and there is little question that households constitute a major sector of production of goods and services.

S. Burns presents data for the U.S. which show much the same result. But of great interest are the historical data presented. In 1900, annual capital investment in the household equaled only 35 percent that of industry, but by 1960 household investment was 110 percent that of industry. Burns concludes that sometime during the 1950s industrial America no longer was the center of capital formation and investment. Instead, the household became the focus of capital formation.[35]

This U.S. trend corroborates the data and thesis presented by J. Gershuny for the U.K.[36] His thesis is that in industrial countries the household is increasingly providing more of its own services, such as domestic help, laundry, home entertainment, transportation--services that were formerly purchased in the formal economy. Consequently, the purchase of consumer durables rises to produce these services. Of the household expenditure allocated to domestic help, laundry, entertainment and transport, Gershuny estimates that in 1954, 56 percent of the expenditure was used to purchase these services in the market, and 44 percent was devoted to household durables to produce the services at home. By 1974, these respective percentages had changed to 20 percent and 80 percent, thus indicating the growth of the self-service economy and the increasing importance of household durables in it.

The Underground Economy

Although the underground or black economy is not a part of the informal economy as we have defined it, there is enough interest in the former to warrant a look at the available data on its size.[37] Readers must be cautioned at the outset that estimates of underground activity are quite crude and vary considerably from researcher to researcher and according to the method used, and that definitions of the underground are not uniform either. For the most part, however, what is being measured is the amount of economic activity involving the exchange of money, but which is not recorded by tax or national account (GNP) authorities. The most popular method is one or another variation of estimating how much the use of currency has increased relative to GNP and bank deposits. Since currency is the primary method of payment within the underground economy, an "abnormal" increase in its use is taken as a measure of its growth. Based on this type of roundabout research, the following estimates have been arrived at during recent years.[38]

There have been three well-known studies conducted in the U.S. A government study by the Internal Revenue Service for 1976 reported that the underground economy ranged in value between 8-10 percent of GNP. Two academic studies give widely divergent results. The first (by Gutmann) estimated underground activity to equal about 10 percent of GNP in 1976. The later study by Edgar Feige estimated the value of underground activity to be 19 percent of GNP in 1976 and 27 percent in 1978--a startling growth rate that has been strongly challenged by others.

When Feige applied the same method to the British economy, he concluded that underground activity was equal to about 15 percent of GNP in 1978. Two different government studies, however, come up with much lower rates. The Central Statistical Office study estimates the value of underground activity to be about 3 percent of GNP, while the Internal Revenue study places its size at 6-7 percent of GNP.

The single estimate derived for Canada emanates from an academic study which used both the Gutmann and Feige procedures. This study found the value of underground activity to be between 10-15 percent of GNP in 1981 (equivalent to between $33 and $49 billion). The authors concluded that this level of activity may be supporting as many as 150,000 full-time jobs.

Summary: How Much Unmeasured?

How much informal activity recorded in this chapter escaped inclusion in the hallowed GNP accounts? It is safe to assume that most small business and self-employed activity is recorded. Some major exceptions, however, would be the unpaid labor input of spouses and other family members into family enterprises, especially farms.

Likewise, much cooperative and collective activity would also be picked up by GNP accountants. However, in most small co-ops, members make time contributions which result in lower prices to the members. These lower prices would be reflected in the GNP accounts as a lower volume of business, and no imputed wage adjustment would be made to reflect the efforts of the co-op members. Consequently, GNP is bound to understate the economic contribution of co-ops and collectives, especially the smaller ones.

With respect to community enterprise activity, much is excluded in the GNP but certainly not all. For example, under the Local Initiatives Program (LIP), a former federal direct job-creation program, no activity was recorded because payments were regarded as transfers like old-age pensions, social assistance and unemployment insurance. But economic production was occurring and not being recorded by GNP.

Much more serious, however, is the exclusion of an implicit

evaluation of the labor and goods volunteered to community enterprises and organizations. Time, church basements, baking, painting, laundering and so on are donated to community organizations in considerable volume, but will never be calculated in GNP.

The proportion of the village economy which consists of domestic production and mutual aid is omitted from the GNP, and so also are household activity, barter and skills exchange. The only exceptions to this are commercial barter, imputed evaluations of owner-occupied housing and some adjustment for home-produced food consumed by farmers.

There will always be too many methodological problems to construct an agreed-on measure of all economic activity. Frankly, we doubt it would be worth the effort. But what seems clear is that by simply calculating much of the activity that is now excluded, and using present GNP accounting methods, GNP would rise considerably. By how much? The only firm estimates are for household production, which would add 40 percent to GNP. Then, by adding in mutual aid, volunteered time and goods, some community organizational activity and unpaid labor in small businesses and co-ops, it seems reasonable to believe that the unrecorded and legal (most of it informal) part of our economy would be at least one-half of recorded GNP.

CHAPTER SIX

POLICY IMPLICATIONS

The current attention being focused on the illegal underground economy has made economic policy makers aware of a considerable amount of economic activity falling outside their area of analysis and policy impact. However, while a certain amount of concern and discussion surrounds this illegal economic activity--equal to perhaps 10-15 percent of GNP--there seems to be little concern or recognition of all the informal but legal economic activity--equal to perhaps 50 percent of GNP--that also mostly falls outside of the policy maker's purview.

Probably the recession and its accompanying high levels of recorded unemployment are playing a role in the revived interest in informal economic activities. Certainly, in towns dominated by single industries and having drastically curtailed employment, new economic initiatives can be found. Consumer and worker cooperatives and skills exchanges are springing up. Extensive efforts are being made to create new types of diverse enterprises with strong community and small-business bases, and in several communities thriving community development corporations are providing a mixture of goods and services. As well, one reads almost weekly of attempts by workers to take over and manage --through a private/public consortium--plants that have not been able to generate enough commercial profit for their often absentee owners, but which can still generate enough social benefit to justify their continuation.

Studies and news reports have also documented that the recession has meant, in some cases, a restructuring of household productive activities. Males, laid off from jobs that were formerly considered secure, are now performing increased household, child-rearing and community work, while wives are seeking part-time paid work for the first time. In all of the above cases throughout Canada, it is too early to tell whether the recession, if turned around, will lead to a return to former economic patterns--or whether once tried, albeit out of necessity, the new economic and social patterns will persist.

If policy makers are concerned that the illegal underground economy is damaging their forecasts and policy prescriptions, then they should be even more alarmed with these legitimate ways that people are engaging in economic activity outside traditional areas. This activity should not be ignored. It should be better understood by policy makers and incorporated into their theories, forecasts and policy advice; it should be better understood by all of us.

If perhaps the equivalent of as much as 50 percent of recorded GNP is conducted legally outside of traditional accounting frameworks, we cannot simply focus on GNP and its derivatives as performance indicators and honestly claim to be developing current policy responses for the entire economy. What is clearly missing is one-third of the nation's total economic activity.

To implicitly behave as if the formal economy and its values represent all economic activity assumes in traditional macroeconomic analysis and accounting procedures that informal economic activity is similar in nature to, and highly correlated with, movements in formal economic activity. Therefore, what is true of formal activity is true of informal. Unfortunately, this assumption is wrong, and bad policy is generated because of it.

For example, in recent years, it has been a common policy of governments to restrain and depress the formal economy in order to cool down inflationary pressures. It has also been a complementary policy in these same countries to restrain and depress social payments which represent important financial supports for informal activity. But policy should not treat both types of activity alike in this situation. Informal production provides the most important safety net society has when the formal economy is depressed. And this activity should be supported (through social payments), not reduced during recessionary periods through budget cut-backs.

By depressing social payments and weakening healthy informal activity, policy makers seem to be assuming that there is also inflation in the informal economy which has to be cooled down by restraint. However, such is not likely to be the case since money and prices are generally not used, or used as much, in informal activity. But implicitly, policy makers have decreed that what is good medicine for formal activity is also good for informal.

By looking at the whole economy--that is, activity in all the four quadrants as outlined in Chapter Four--policy makers and politicians could avoid making this type of serious error. We should understand that one type of activity (informal) could replace others (formal) and that legal forms of informal economic activity should be encouraged, not discouraged, in order to attack inflation in the formal sector. By focusing on all legal forms of economic activity, policies to manage the economy would also make explicit what an increasing number of economists and others are now beginning to acknowledge: that economic and social forces are closely linked, even though the formulation of policies and the monitoring of policy performance tend to separate the social and economic spheres in most industrialized countries.

To take an example, the influx of women into the job market in recent years is as much attributable to social forces as it is to economic. Yet, topics such as female participation rates and equal wages are considered purely economic and dealt with almost entirely within a traditional supply and demand framework. Policy makers seldom stop to examine why such a fundamental shift in the labor market is taking place, or whether solutions other than trying to provide more "jobs" in the traditional sectors through subsidies, export development, tax incentives, industrial strategies and the like--with all the attendant high costs to society and particular social impacts--are more appropriate.

A whole economy (holistic) perspective would see this fundamental change in the labor market as a shift among the quadrants of economic activity, motivated by economic (largely pay) and social (largely personal and human development) forces. With this broader perspective, issues could be addressed such as: the small direct financial rewards attached to most informal activity (chiefly within the household); why women dominate the informal sector; why men perform the greatest share of the well-paid formal activities; and how, perhaps through job sharing and an improved income transfer system, we could bring about a better distribution of activities among males and females and a more equal system of rewards.

A whole economy perspective applied to this social shift would not in itself guarantee easy solutions, but it would encourage us to look at a much broader range of options. Now we simply look at the choice between either artificially stimu-lating more traditional jobs, or failing this, providing social assistance and unemployment benefits which increase dependency on governments and do little to encourage self-reliance because of their regulations and conditions. The ultimate and proper task of economic policy should be to determine the mix of formal and informal economic activity a society wants and provide the incentives and encouragement required to support this balance. Because informal activity has a high humanistic and social content (based on its social accounting rationale), encouraging more of it will go a long way towards integrating economic and social policies in the process. In effect, households and communities will have an economic base from which they can effectively and collectively "privatize" many social service functions now performed by government. However, note that this transfer of a social obligation to the community will only succeed if enhanced informal economic activity is first supported and encouraged. Presently, there seems to be much wishful thinking among some conservative politicians that social obligations can just be thrown back upon the community without any change in economic structures.

Seeking a New Balance of Economic Activity

In developing the economy we do not see informal activity as an alternative to or replacement for all current formal activity. But we believe that more of our economic and social needs should be met through increased informal activity. It is through greater informal activity that people seeking more social and human ways of relating to one another will have an opportunity to express these ways. This is due to the small size of informal structures and the fact that their activity is founded on social accounting. An expansion of informal activity, which is highly labor-intensive, is also a more appropriate and cheaper solution for providing work opportunities, rather than attempting to provide all opportunities through expanded employment in the capital-intensive formal sector.

Historically, we have witnessed a movement towards bigness and commercial accounting. Small units, which formerly undertook some activities, have been driven out of business or agglomerated by larger ones. Activities which were once done informally in the household and neighborhood have been, to varying degrees, abandoned to the marketplace where commercial profit is the rationale. These latter activities include food growing, meal preparation, day care, education, home, car, appliance repair and so forth. What we once produced ourselves we now purchase generally from large units.

Within this overall trend there has also been some movement away from big business towards big government. This trend was designed to reduce the shortcomings of so much activity being guided by a commercial accounting rationale in favor of collective social accounting. However, the results have been diminished, and in some cases perverse, because the decisions were made by large public units. The intent was good, but the large structures dictated unsatisfactory results. Consequently, disenchanted with big liberal governments, the conservative trend has been to turn back and privatize much public activity. But this may lead to big business running more of our affairs and nothing much will have changed.

The accompanying Figure 5 can be used to easily demonstrate overall policy objectives:

FIGURE 5

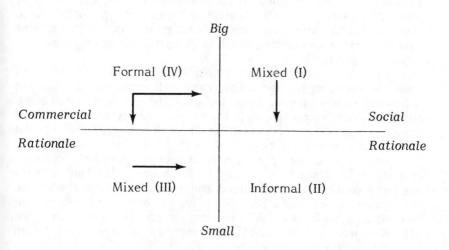

The proposed changes can be summarized:

(i) More large formal activity (IV) would be downscaled where possible and located in III. Other large-scale activities where downscaling is not practical could be moved closer to the vertical axis or into I. This latter movement implies only that large private corporate units would now pay more attention to social accounting. It does not imply nationalization or crown corporation status, although this might occur in some cases.

(ii) Large-scale public sector activity (I) would be downscaled through devolution. This means more decisions would be made by local and community governments. In the 1970s, the provincial government of British Columbia experimented with devolution by establishing community resource boards in Vancouver. It was hoped these local boards would eventually permit community groups to develop more appropriate responses to certain needs such as education and social services.

Unfortunately, before this exciting process could mature, a more authoritarian government terminated it. Imperfect but promising federal job-creation projects based on local initiative, such as the Local Initiatives Program (LIP), Opportunities for Youth (OFY), Local Employment Assistance Program (LEAP) and Canada Works were examples of how control could begin to be downsized and returned to the community. The delegation of greater authority by the federal government to Indian band councils and Native communities is another example, although this case illustrates the further need to transfer resources as well as formal authority.

(iii) Some small-scale commercial enterprises located in III may be encouraged to adopt more of a social accounting rationale. For example, more aid could be given to small-scale activities such as co-ops, collectives, community enterprises and voluntary activity. Not all small business need be of the traditional commercial type.

(iv) The majority of past and present informal economic activity in quadrant II is located in the household. This activity has been continually downvalued and taken for granted with the result that it has withered. Some males' new-found interest in household activity and child-rearing, in combination with more effective work-sharing and social security arrangements, could turn this sector around in the future.

Figure 6 illustrates the type of change that would result in the configuration of all economic activity if the above four changes occurred:

FIGURE 6

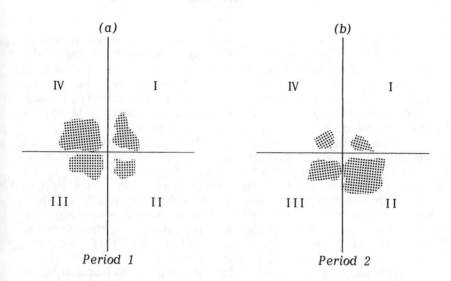

(a)   (b)

Period 1   Period 2

It should be noted that by moving more economic activity towards the informal sector, we are automatically linking economic and social concerns.   If informal economic activity addresses the human and social consequences of production, we no longer need to talk about distinct "social" and "economic" policies. Nor do we need to discuss social policy as a residual of economic policy to be addressed separately by the state after the economic system has run its course.

Finally, if the informal economy heeds the human and social effects of production, we can no longer consider that the economic sector pays the bill for costly social programs.   Economic and social policy will tend to become one and the same, and we can talk about the "social economy."

In conclusion to seeking a new balance, there are many factors that wittingly and unwittingly perpetuate formal activity and resist shifts to more informal economic activity--the bias of our influential economic output measures, the bias of traditional concepts of work and employment practices, outdated public revenue and expenditure systems and the glorification of specialization and the competitive international economy.

The Bias Given to Formal Economic Activity
by GNP and Related Output Measures

Economic development policies, such as whether to stimulate or restrain the economy, are based on the performance of the formal economy (and more precisely on those statistics used to monitor it, such as GNP, exports, paid employment and productivity). If an increasing amount of economic activity is being undertaken outside the formal economy, this activity is beyond the purview of the leading economic statistics.

One of the untested statements frequently voiced is that because more and more people are working in the informal economy (as well as performing illegal activities) the recent and current recessions are not fomenting as much observable unrest as the high unemployment rates might otherwise predict. It is certainly likely that our official economic measures overstate the true extent of both upswings and downswings in the economy. Much of what happens is simply a shift between formal (recorded) and informal (unrecorded) activity--a substitution of one type of economic activity for another--but only the formal activity gets recorded. What the net increase or decrease in activity is cannot be accurately related by our present indicators.

The main concern for policy makers is determining to what extent the presumed formerly reliable economic performance indicators can be used. The GNP measure has a lot of well-known shortcomings, most of which are associated with its inability to differentiate between current economic activity that originates from "goods" production--food, steel, TVs, etc.--and that which originates from the growth of "bads"--cancer treatment, crime prevention and so on. All of this activity is lumped together through the use of dollar values and accorded equal merit or quality. Thus, GNP is never given very high marks as being useful as a welfare measure, even though it is often used as such in making international and intertemporal comparisons.

At this juncture, it is helpful to understand what activities GNP includes and excludes.[1] In Canada, the development of a comprehensive national accounting system is fairly recent and only since the end of the '40s have regular GNP estimates been available in Canada.

GNP technically includes all current productive activity in the private sector that results in exchanges of money, e.g., salaries, wages, profit, rent, interest. It also includes similar activities pursued by governments. The key criteria for activities to be included in GNP are "current," "money" and "produced in Canada" (imports are excluded). If a good that was produced and sold last year is resold this year, it is not included. A good that was never exchanged for money is excluded. Also, an attempt is made to put a value on items such as the home-grown food that farmers (but not others) consume, room and board provided for employees and an imputed shelter allowance ("rent") for owner-occupied houses. For accounting purposes all other consumer durables are assumed to depreciate completely within the year they are produced, and hence provide no satisfaction or welfare.

By focusing only on current productive activity, GNP discriminates against durability and secondhand goods. Automobiles or refrigerators replaced annually by new models are added to GNP, whereas used autos and fridges recycled through formal or informal secondhand markets are not. Even though recycled secondhand goods produce considerable utility and welfare to their owners, they are not considered to be the result of current productive activity. While secondhand goods are excluded in theory from the GNP, in practice it is very difficult to do so, and with the exception of the sales of used cars, most formalized secondhand economic activity involving money exchange does end up being counted. Goods traded informally never enter GNP.

As long as it is understood that GNP is only a measure of current activity (or "busyness"), then this accounting practice of excluding the value produced by used goods can be defended. But a problem arises when GNP is used as a measure of a country's welfare, which it often is. For example, on an international basis the United Nations uses it to measure need among the countries of the world, and it is frequently used to compare the gains in "welfare" over time within a country. Obviously, if recycled used goods are excluded, GNP can only be at best a partial measure of a country's welfare.

Because of this overriding concern with activity directed towards exchange ("busyness") rather than with welfare, a lot of "bads" are mixed in with goods production in calculating GNP. If crime rises, then police activity also rises and GNP goes up. If industrial activity leads to increased pollution, only the goods produced and not the disservices created are accounted for in GNP. But when the pollution is cleared up, this activity is also added in. In fact, the many costs associated with pollution—health, financial, aesthetic—should properly be deducted from the value of GNP if it is to serve as a welfare measure. These costs are a negative consequence or output of industrial activity, not a benefit.

To take another example, if automobile production and consumption rise and this leads to more accidents and rising health costs, these activities too are included in GNP. Again, like pollution costs, they should be deducted or netted out from GNP if welfare is being measured. In conclusion, because GNP concentrates on measuring activity and makes no welfare or qualitative judgement about the nature of the activity, when GNP changes we are never certain whether it is the result of a change in the production of goods or "bads." A sure way to increase GNP under present accounting rules would be to build unsafe cars so that the resulting health and property repair activity (cost) would swell GNP!

Of great importance from the standpoint of reflecting informal economic activity is the kinds of activities the GNP measure excludes. In terms of our earlier four quadrants of economic activity, there are four types of activity almost wholly excluded from GNP--voluntary activity, mutual assistance, non-commercial barter and skills exchange and household activity. Exclusion of voluntary activity is defended by statisticians on the basis that it is not paid for and, therefore, difficult to measure. Whatever the statistical rationale, the exclusion of voluntary activity means that in Canada about a quarter of a million person-years of labor activity has not been accounted for in recent years. In comparative terms, the volunteer labor force is equal in size to the combined employed labor forces of Saskatoon, Regina and Victoria, three of Canada's medium-sized cities. And while we would be suspicious of a measure of Canada's economic activity or welfare if it excluded these three cities, this is exactly what GNP does the equivalent of by excluding voluntary activity.

Mutual aid, bartering, skill exchanges and so on also reflect economic activity excluded from GNP. If you prepare your neighbor's tax return and she or he repairs your driveway this does not enter into GNP. If you both hire the necessary professionals to do the work then it enters GNP. But notice that in both cases the same amount of work and final output occurs.

Even more paradoxical is what happens in the first case if the neighbors had exchanged $100 for their services. Neither would be out of pocket financially, the work would be done as before, but now the mutual activity enters GNP. The exchange of money itself creates the mistaken impression that $200 worth of additional activity has been performed when, in fact, no additional economic activity has occurred except the passing back and forth of $100. Perhaps it is no wonder that we so often confuse money with value. (This example assumes that neither party engages in these activities as a business, in which case they could be accused of failing to record and report taxable income.)

The biggest sector neglected by GNP is household activity. Here again, the reason for this neglect is the alleged statistical difficulty of measuring unpaid household labor. But mainstream economic textbooks defend the exclusion of about one-third of all economic activity with little expressed concern by adding a rather standard disclaimer: so long as the value of these services does not change much, the variation in GNP will provide a reasonably accurate picture of the variation in total output.[2]

There are two fundamental shortcomings with this type of complacent disclaimer which reveal much about the biases of mainstream economics. First, even a casual examination of the changing structure of household activity in the past 25 years would suggest that something has changed. The number of single-parent households has risen, the number of two-family households has fallen, household technological innovation has increased dramatically, households today are more urbanized, there are more two-earner households and so forth. Surely, these changes should lead even a slightly curious accountant to reject the notion that "as long as there have been no changes we can use the traditional GNP measure," when all about us we see nothing but change.

This nonchalance leads to the second shortcoming. If it is assumed that nothing has changed in the household sector then, of course, there is no temptation to investigate it. If as much time and resources were showered on the household sector as on the manufacturing sector, accountants would likely find the household a very exciting and important locus of economic activity. There are 30,000 manufacturing establishments in Canada compared with over eight million households. If one searches Statistics Canada publications he or she finds the minutest details on manufacturing activity in Canada recorded on a monthly basis, but very little on household economic activity, and even then usually only on a decennial census basis. Yet, most estimates would place the contributions of the manufacturing and household sectors to a country's total economic activity as roughly of the same magnitude.

If, as the result of disclaimers and traditional male attitudes, we do not include household (largely female) activity in

GNP, that is still only a measurement problem, and perhaps not a crucial matter. But unfortunately there are graver consequences: the absence of measurement inevitably leads to an undervaluation of the activity, as well as of the people who perform it. If household workers received the same status, rights and rewards as their industrial counterparts, they would probably feel indifferent to their exclusion from GNP. But such is not the case in industrial societies.

Perhaps the following anecdote best sums up the effects of slighting the value of household activity and the dominant male attitude towards it. In 1973, a male British magistrate's practice of sentencing those committing minor misdemeanors to clean up old age pensioner's apartments drew the following comment from a female reporter on a London paper:

> It may come as a surprise to the magistrate that thousands of women in this country are interned for varying periods of time, week in and week out, performing the new ultimate deterrent known as "housework." Many are finding it increasingly difficult to remember what offense they committed in the first place.[3]

The second important consequence of excluding household activity from GNP is that it overstates the past growth of net economic activity in Canada. Historically, there has been a continuous shift of activity away from the household and community into the formal GNP sector (for example, food preparation, fuel provision, home construction, child care, care of the aged, entertainment, etc.). But because GNP only adds in the formal activity and does not adjust downwards for reduced informal activity, these shifts have all been interpreted as net gains in economic activity.

Are the people, especially women, performing this increased formal activity, reducing or altering their economic activity elsewhere? A family meal at McDonald's restaurant is often a substitute for a home-prepared meal and this reduced household meal preparation should be deducted from the nation's total of economic activity. Unfortunately, the present construction of the national accounts does not permit a determination of whether total economic activity has risen or fallen in the past, since much of this newly measured activity simply represents a shift between sectors.

The solution to monitoring economic activity more accurately would not seem to lie in reworking GNP. To try to convert all unrecorded economic activity into dollars as if it went through the marketplace not only presents a very difficult measurement problem, both empirically and conceptually, but also a fundamental problem as to whether the qualitative differences in such activities as parental child care versus institutional child care can be captured by a dollar value. Is a dollar's worth of child care identical regardless of how it is performed (produced)?

If people undertake productive activities for social as well as output (strictly economic) reasons, then it seems inappropriate to monitor that activity only by its output (dollar) component. An output or strictly economic measure is appropriate for profit-maximizing, efficiency-striving commercial firms, where the human consequences of production are relatively unimportant. But when other motivations are at the base of, or complementary to production (output), then an economic measure alone is no longer appropriate.

An important economic indicator related to GNP is "productivity," a measure obtained by simply dividing dollar output by the number of employed person-hours required to produce the output. While technically this measure should be called labor productivity, the word "labor" is generally overlooked, and it is now commonplace to use the phrase productivity to imply a measure of total productivity. Moreover, economists have not developed an acceptable operational measure of overall productivity, so labor productivity frequently, and sometimes unintentionally, becomes the proxy for a total productivity measure.

The major shortcoming of this partial productivity measure when it is used as an indicator of the economy's health ("top economist claims recovery is on the way because productivity is up," etc.) is that it implicitly assumes productivity is only affected by the performance of labor. But, in fact, the numerator in this index--output--is clearly related to the contributions of all factors of production (land, labor, capital) and how effectively they are organized (management). A keen and well-trained labor force working with poor equipment, bad space and poor management will have lower productivity than a slack labor force working with superior factors of production and brilliantly managed. Nevertheless, the easiest and often cheapest way to increase productivity is to reduce the labor hours in the denominator. This is done by introducing more capital such as robots and computers into the work process. Hence, this productivity measure also has a built-in capital-investment bias.

The productivity measure is too incomplete, imprecise and

misleading to be of much use other than as a motherhood phrase: who could possibly be against productivity? Because productivity can be increased by various methods, not all of which are efficient or acceptable, an increase in output per person-hour is not necessarily a healthy development. For example, an output of $200 could be produced, let us say, by 10 persons working a total of 10 hours at $1 an hour, and productivity would be equal to a value of 2 ($200/100 hours). Now we could increase productivity by buying $500 worth of equipment from Japan, and reducing the labor force and hours worked from 100 hours to 20 hours while total output remains the same. But productivity ($200/20 hours) rises to a value of 10.

In theory, we should now rejoice--productivity has increased fivefold. But whether we are better off as a community is questionable and complicated to calculate. First, it was necessary to expend more money to secure the increased productivity--we had to buy the machines to replace the labor. Secondly, we imported the machines from Japan so now we may face a balance-of-payments problem and a fall in the value of the dollar. Third, we may have created unemployment as a result of the reduced labor requirements. Finally, if the layoff of workers is substantial and the firm is a significant employer in the region, we may have a disruption in community life.

The next time someone observes that we must raise productivity in order to increase the standard of living, ask them whose standard of living, exactly how they propose to do it and what will be the human consequences within the community? To be sure, private profits may rise and output may rise and this will satisfy some business people and economists, but this does not mean that the well-being of the community will rise--which is what we are led to believe.

In the final analysis, policy, decisions based on GNP and related output measures used for monitoring a nation's economic activity are incomplete and too narrowly economic. And perhaps worst of all, they give enhanced status to formal economic activity while downgrading informal. These shortcomings suggest the adoption of more comprehensive measures along the lines of social indicators or impact-asessment techniques. Ultimately, we must develop procedures that allow economic decisions to be made collectively, but democratically, which reflect what is appropriate to the community's needs. More important than developing sophisticated indicators is developing structures that will fulfill the conditions of informal production--small-scale and a social accounting rationale.

Biases of Our Concepts of Work
and Employment Practices

The continuing use of traditional employment concepts, coupled with a growing number of people opting for full- or part-time informal activity, means that an increasing number of people will routinely become classed as "unemployed" or "underemployed," even though they may be working but not employed full time.

Unfortunately, the terms "employment" and "work" in industrialized societies have become over time almost synonymous in their usage. If people are not employed they are not working. The most galling question that can be asked of a housewife is "do you work"--meaning are you employed? Similarly, many Native people in the North who hunt, fish, cut wood and repair their own engines would be classified in a typical government employment survey as unemployed, even though they work very hard and produce things of essential value. Although the relationship is weakening, work is still confused with employment and, more specifically, paid employment. Not to be paid is to be thought of as not productive and not working and, consequently, as having no economic value and no legitimate claim to income. And this is the shame the unemployed are made to feel even though they may be heavily engaged in informal activity and self-dependency. But in commercial society informal activity is largely unrecognized and unvalued--mostly, we view it as leisure or as a hobby.

We should begin our rethinking of work and income by clarifying what is meant by terms such as "work," "employment," "unemployment," "labor force" and "wages."[4] Under the current meanings of these words people not lucky enough to find employment, and hence a legitimate income, are being relegated to a peripheral position in society and a life of subsistence on inadequate transfer payments. In this structure they are frequently seen as "living off" society.

Looking at work activity across the spectrum of the whole economy should permit agreement on a much wider definition of work--formal and informal, remunerated and unremunerated. Activities could then be remunerated according to a new set of rules arrived at collectively. Employment policy would focus on the whole range of economic activity with an eye to a proper balance of activities, a proper distribution among society's members and proper remuneration for the different activities. This is the only real meaning of "full employment" within the wide spectrum of society's economic activities.

On the other hand, the continued neglect of much informal economic activity will lead to more and more people living on inadequate transfer payments, being restricted in their activities by regulations attached to the payments, becoming dependent on the system and, in many cases, creating costly social problems as a consequence of this enforced meagre standard of living.

Turning away from work and income concepts, there are also significant implications of our approach to employment policies. There will be a need to reorient a whole range of policies (for example, counseling, job creation, training) towards personal, household and community enterprise initiatives and away from the emphasis on employment in large commercial enterprises.

There are few instances in our employment policies where one is encouraged and assisted in developing individual and community-based entrepreneurship. The attitude found at employment centers is "find a job," become an employee, become more dependent. There should be greater emphasis on "creating a job" and developing self-reliance and on working with others as a team to create community enterprises. Other than sporadic and stop-go attempts at local initiative projects, employment officials in most industrialized countries encourage applicants at employment centers to consider opportunities only in the formalized commercial sector of the economy. Contrary to what is commonly heard today, the work ethic is far from dead--but perhaps the employment ethic is dying.

The types of economic activities that people could create with some encouragement may be hard to imagine since we have long been encouraged to think of megaprojects and the promised employment of thousands of people. It seems easier to get the government to put up $100 million to save the jobs of 1,500 employees in one plant, than it is to put $10 million into the creation of 1,000 small enterprises that would eventually create work for 2,000 people.

With respect to employment creation processes, nowhere are the difficulties in trying to provide for traditional full-employment opportunities better illustrated than through the daily advertisements for jobs in the trendy "information" sector of the formal economy. An advertisement recently placed in a news-paper by a provincial government (which could easily have been placed by any large corporation) spelled out the job descriptions of three positions in the salary range of $30,000-$40,000. One of these descriptions follows:

Supervisor, Production Services: $28,700-$34,200

This is a challenging opportunity with the MINISTRY OF REVENUE, taxpayer services branch, to supervise staff involved in planning, preparing and delivering information packages in all media on ministry programs for taxpayers. You will develop branch communications services and re-commend policy, advertising and distribution strategies; liaise with senior management; guide professional com-munications staff in planning, design and preparation of information materials, major communications proposals and media plans; allocate staff and resources; monitor progress of projects; hire technical consultants on a project basis.

A reading of the "buzz words" in this and the other two job descriptions clearly illustrates the types of activities being played out each day in large private and public hierarchies: "recommend options," "steering committees," "liaise," "review proposals," "task forces," "monitor," "appraise effectiveness," "evaluate," etc. Looking at the job descriptions, one wonders if the major purpose of these jobs is not largely to generate more institutional activity--more phone calls, memos, subcommittees, plane travel --in a perpetual make-work cycle. Do these jobs contribute more (or anything) than they cost society?

Regrettably, these kinds of jobs are of a type which an industrial society feels compelled to improvise in the big business and public sectors in order to keep the system and its people "working" when there is a labor surplus. Because work is equated with employment and income in industrial nations, we are even compelled to invent activity in the public sector that resembles "real" private sector employment (and playing it out in fancy large offices helps) in order to justify the payment of incomes.

Considering the many and increasing microelectronic inno-vations in office work, one wonders what proportion of new jobs created will be of the make-work type. The potential for providing "busy-work" is alarming, and fancying up the status of these jobs by classifying them as part of the emerging "infor-mation" sector will not fool anyone for long.

Since many of these jobholders contribute very little to a nation's output through their employment but frequently receive larger than average salaries, the question arises as to why this surplus income spent on trivial jobs cannot be channeled into avenues that would permit these and other people to perform tasks informally that are of more value to themselves and to society. As more and more people become aware of this breakdown in industrial economies (including the people performing these make-work tasks) perhaps the way the industrial system deploys and rewards people will be seriously challenged.

Some may scoff at the idea of young entrepreneurs today being interested in small businesses, co-ops, community corporations and the like, when much larger rewards can be had in major corporations and government. But one significant factor has changed the calculus of career decision making since the 1950s and 1960s--that is, the nature of the job opportunities available to young people in the 1980s and 1990s. In 1960, a labor force entrant would look at the various alternatives, compare them to "cushy" jobs in a major corporation or in government, and running a small enterprise or community organization would pale in comparison.

Today, fewer of these cushy jobs are around and even the parents of many young labor force entrants are being bounced from what once looked like lifelong employment sinecures. The alternatives to creating a more modest job today (with perhaps a smaller financial reward) are not corporate or government jobs, but unemployment insurance and welfare. Compared to these unattractive alternatives, it is no wonder that more young people are expressing an interest in creating informal, but sustainable, work opportunities on a small scale.

Policy makers should recognize this shift in perspective and begin looking at alternatives that are socially sustainable--if not commercially profitable. UIC benefits and welfare payments do not support or encourage sustainable activities; they are temporary and stop-gap measures devised for earlier times when full employment in the commercial sector prevailed. Community enterprises, small businesses, co-ops, volunteer and household work are all socially sustainable activities that should receive increased support. What is required for creating paid-work opportunities is a change in attitudes and in our accounting methods for determining those activities which ought to receive community support. We need to move from a calculus of commercial profitability to one of social sustainability.

Social costs and benefits are often difficult to determine if great precision is required. But community members usually have little difficulty determining whether the benefits to their community exceed the costs. Without putting precise dollar figures on the costs and benefits, a community knows whether an activity is a net asset or a liability after considering all factors. For example, a small food co-op run by six people may not result in enough business to cover their salaries so it is not commercially profitable. But after the community calculates the savings in unemployment and welfare payments (and a reduction in the other potential and often long-term social costs associated with unemployment) and adds in the social benefits of working, the co-op may very likely be judged a socially sustainable and, hence, a beneficial alternative.

Too often today, unfortunately, businesses or organizations must be judged commercially profitable to survive. If a socially sustainable enterprise goes out of operation and creates unemployment, government deals with the problem after the fact with large, residual social programs to cope with the social costs. But these very expensive programs seldom nourish initiative or create a spirit of self-reliance among persons or communities. In the jargon of health care, a preventive rather than a remedial approach must be adopted by more community social and employment support systems. If not, we will certainly end up with a surplus of very expensive chronic-care patients in the decades ahead.

It is hoped that a down-valuing of formal and an up-valuing of informal activity will enhance the likelihood of more people of both sexes participating more equally in both types of activities. One result should be that males perform more household and community work, while women perform more formal work. More female participation in the formal economy may also transform the male structures and roles prevailing there and to some extent deformalize present economic activity in the formal sector. After this is done, perhaps the "second stage" will be prepared, where, as the American feminist Betty Friedan sees it, males and females share equally in the performance and rewards of employment and household responsibilities.[5]

Encouraging the development and revaluation of informal activity also gives more meaning to the idea of work sharing. Today, work sharing (i.e., less time at formal paid employment) seems unattractive because we have the habit of assuming that any activity off-the-job is "leisure" and unproductive--where leisure is perceived as on TV "with Bill and the boys and their beer" thrashing about in canoes.

But when most of what happens off-the-job is viewed as another form of economic activity then the potential for work sharing is enhanced. We must also face the fact that there is unlikely to be enough 40-hour-a-week, formal economy jobs to go around to satisfy all those who want them, at least at the expected wages. Why not encourage the formal economy jobholders to reduce their work weeks and build their patio decks themselves, to volunteer at the school for a few hours a week, to work a day at the co-op retail store or day-care center, write for the community newspaper or start developing a community development corporation. These are not "down-time" leisure activities; they all represent productive activities that add to household and community well-being. Instead of spending so much of our work time at specialized jobs and using the money for buying our well-being, let us be more direct and reserve more time to produce directly some of these essential items for personal, household and community well-being.

Unfortunately, there are fundamental reasons why people in the formal economy have not been overly interested in devoting more time to informal activity. These fundamental factors will have to be changed before we can expect the development of more informal activity. A major reason is that many persons and households cannot afford, at least in urban areas, to spend more time away from formal activity. We still have the poorest 20 percent of Canadian families taking home only a pitiful 4 percent of total Canadian income--and some of these families have two earners. These families are still struggling to achieve the basic necessities of life, and to advise them that they would enhance their well-being by working for a community newspaper, devoting time to a co-op, starting a collective or non-profit business or volunteering to supervise school recess periods would require a fanciful and romantic imagination. Although all industrialized nations are wealthy enough to provide the basic necessities of life--and then some--to every household, they choose not to do so. If a basic income floor were provided to all households then everybody could make a more deliberate choice concerning the allocation of their time and resources between formal and informal activity.

Another important factor prohibiting withdrawal from the formal economy is that informal activity is undervalued and underrated. Formal work is male and macho--"where the action is"--while informal work is female and sissy. As a result, many informal activities are not encouraged to flourish. For example, raising children is only now being regarded by more people as a work of art, rather than simply something that has to be done by the mother because she is left at home. Hopefully, all informal activities will begin to be seen as worthy satisfying pursuits not only for our daughters but our sons as well. But for this change in perception to develop, we first need to change the way we account for and evaluate economic activity. As already suggested, this means we must change the detrimental role played by GNP and other economic measures that count and value formal activity only.

Industrially Biased Government Revenue and Expenditure Concepts and Policies

Besides the changes required in the work, income and economic indicator areas, adjustments are needed in our revenue and expenditure systems. The major source of government revenue is taxes, and a major implication of a significant shift to informal activity is the erosion of the tax base, particularly income and sales taxes.

Our entire tax system is based on income, prices and the use of money. If these factors become less important, then a tax system based on them will also become less important. On the one hand, if an increasing amount of economic activity is not facilitated by wages and prices and the exchange of money, governments will collect less revenue under presently constructed income and sales tax systems and the ability to match expenditures will fall, or else large deficits or tax increases will be inevitable.

On the expenditure side, it will also become increasingly difficult to allocate public resources, especially income transfers, since income levels are often employed as a measure of need. If people receive more of their needed goods and services and sustain their standards of living through non-cash informal means, it becomes increasingly inaccurate to measure living standards or levels of need by looking at income levels.

The major question here, and the one most urgently confronting governments, is: At what level and on what basis should public goods and services be provided to people who opt for increased informal economic production, when those who support these public services under the present tax constructs are those who participate more heavily in the formal commercial economy? Are taxes dead?

Several issues need to be investigated before a resolution of this issue can be reached. Do people, households and communities which rely heavily on informal activities and, consequently, on themselves require as great a provision of public goods and services as those who are primarily engaged in the formal economy? After all, informal activity, by definition, takes into account social concerns that are often neglected, or are even generated, by formal activity leading to expensive, remedial social programs. Finally, should present tax and funding constructs take priority over the development of informal activity? That is, should informal activity be either discouraged or channeled in a way that the present tax constructs can be made to work, or should the tax and funding system be radically altered to accommodate the realities of emerging new forms of work?

There are basically three resolutions to the tax funding dilemma. First, discourage or declare illegal most informal activity, at least that part not involving money. This, however, would seem impossible both for philosophical and operational reasons. Secondly, by using implicit incomes and prices ("shadow pricing"), an attempt would be made to estimate the amount of informal activity and then it would be subjected to taxation. This also represents an impossibility. In the first instance, measuring the dollar value of activity is conceptually arbitrary, as well as difficult and expensive to accomplish operationally. In the second instance, people participating in many informal activities generate little or no cash with which to pay taxes. This option would serve only to drive legitimate and necessary non-monetized activity underground.

The third approach is to encourage informal activity to develop and radically restructure the tax system. Sweden is an example of a country where the possibility of radical change is being investigated. There, the idea of citizens providing time and effort to governments in lieu of tax payments is being examined. Although this third approach represents a general possibility, it also presents numerous issues, and perhaps after investigation radical change will not prove feasible. Acceptable solutions won't be easy to find, but if informal activity grows it will require serious rethinking about the public funding of goods and services.

Adjustments also will need to be made to the expenditure and income transfer side of the tax system. Many income security constructs and policies are founded on the belief that people, households and communities should be encouraged to devote most of their working time to the formal economy. In days past when labor shortages inhibited industrial growth, the practice of developing industry-biased, social security policies may have been valid from a strict economic standpoint. These policy biases, which encouraged the maximum potential supply of (male) labor for the formal economy, included: the provision of social assistance and public pension benefits at bare subsistence levels to discourage loafing; unemployment benefit regulations set to discourage serious informal activity since workers are placed at the beck and call of the employment office upon immediate notice; and pension and unemployment assistance (as well as the value of fringe benefits) which are often regulated by public statute--all of which scale their benefits positively to the amount of time spent in the formal economy.

In times of relative labor shortage, few people questioned the wisdom of these biases in our income transfer, social security and fringe benefit policies. In an industrial society, industrial concepts riddle our structures and institutional behavior. But during a protracted period of labor surplus, and when increasing numbers of people and communities are expressing an interest in informal economic activity, industrially biased approaches to social security make little sense. It is certainly correct to conclude that present transfer and social security concepts and practices are part of the overall adjustment problem we face, and not part of the solution.

It must be kept in mind that much informal activity can flourish only if some cash flow and material support is available to help sustain it in a healthy state. These support payments should not be seen as a "drag" on the formal economy. Rather, they should be recognized as an active component of overall economic policy that keeps alive an enormous amount of economic activity and also leads to an overall reduction in money spent on expensive, remedial social programs. These so-called social supports should more accurately be seen as "economic incentives," which is what public payments are called when they support economic activity in the formal sector.

A new approach to a transfer program recently taken in France should be watched closely. Under a changed program of unemployment benefits, eligible recipients can obtain their entitled benefits in a lump sum if they agree to establish small enterprises. This type of program change illustrates how current social security benefits could be more creatively channeled in order to encourage individual and community initiative. Similar creative changes in many of our transfer and social security programs could also be made to encourage individual and community initiative in informal ways, rather than encouraging them to wait for the "system" to find them a job.

The Glorification of Specialization and International Competitiveness: The One-Company Town and the One-Skill Household

Nanaimo, British Columbia, and Sudbury and Windsor in Ontario are company towns all suffering the economic and social effects of cut-backs and closures of their main industry. Those who wish to argue that this is only a temporary set-back caused by the worldwide recession may want to look closer at the depressed conditions in Cape Breton, Nova Scotia, with its lingering problems derived from an earlier dependency on coal and steel.

A nation's economic dependency and vulnerability to other nations is generally expressed by its volume of exports and imports of goods and services and its balance of trade. Few economists make judgements concerning how "exposed" a nation should be to other countries through their external trading. Whether a nation exports and imports 5 or 50 percent of its goods and services (GNP) seems to be of limited interest.

What is of interest is whether imports and exports balance. If a nation imports 20 percent of its needs, but only exports 15 percent of its production, then an adverse balance of trade arises (a trading deficit). A country must borrow externally to cover this imbalance, making it clear that it is dependent on persons and events beyond its borders, and causing it to lose some of its sovereignty. If things get out of hand, perhaps the International Monetary Fund (IMF), acting as the banker to nations, will even dictate what a country's future economic policy will be. This has happened to many countries in the past few years, most recently to Mexico, but not long ago to highly industrialized Britain as well.

Until a continued and persistent imbalance occurs, the actual level of trade a country is engaged in is ignored. Mainstream economics and commercial policy in general tend to promote the concepts of free trade and specialization. A nation should be allowed and encouraged to do what it does best, and if it produces too much of something for domestic consumption, it should export the surplus in exchange for things other countries are specializing in and producing a surplus of.

In theory (the theory of "comparative advantage"), this principle works to maximize a nation's economic welfare. But it is a static theory because if some event occurs abroad--a change in government, a war, a new mineral discovery--or if conditions change at home--a rise in wages over time or a depletion of natural resources--then what was commercially profitable yesterday is not today. In these cases, one can see that the extent of international exposure is important. The greater the level of trade, balanced or otherwise, the greater the likelihood that something which happens abroad will disrupt production and people's lives at home.

As the theory goes in the fluid world of international economics, however, all this disruption will be accommodated by the market. Capital and resources will move into new, commercially profitable pursuits, and labor will pick up new jobs, perhaps after retraining and/or moving to another town or region. Incomes may increase or decrease. Certainly, a small balloon exporting firm in Toronto may cut back expenses to accommodate business, in the way the theory predicts, without too much disruption of people's lives. But it is a different matter when an entire town or region, heavily dependent on a major industry, is adversely affected by changes in trade relations.

This brief explanation of what happens to overly exposed nations can be used to examine the trading relationships of communities (or regions) and households. We seldom look at the economics of communities and households in terms of exports and imports and balance of trade. But what is true for nations is also true for smaller trading groups, and it helps illustrate how overspecialization not only makes nations vulnerable and dependent but communities and households as well.

As long as economic and political conditions remain stable or favorable beyond the trading unit, everything appears fine and conventional economic theory works. It is only when external conditions change adversely, as now, that people begin to question their trading relationships and begin to wonder whether they did not trade off too much control over their lives for temporary growth in their material standards of living.

Cities like Nanaimo, Sudbury and Windsor, and regions such as Cape Breton in Nova Scotia, did question these things and saw (with hindsight) that they had overspecialized in their trading relationships with the outside world, both within and beyond Canada's borders. Workers devoted their working days to producing goods and extracting resources for export outside the city or region, and with the money earned bought the imported goods they needed to live on. It seems little care was taken to develop a diversified economic base--a more informal base--which could have satisfied many of these needs locally, and which would have counterbalanced the dependency created by the dominant industry. People in these cities worked *in* the community but not *for* it, and especially not for one another.

In Windsor's heyday, auto carriers, leaving the city loaded down with new cars for Toronto 250 miles away, passed trucks loaded with bread heading for Windsor. As Windsor rebuilds its economy today, it needs to look for people or organizations who can produce baked goods locally, who can establish locally owned hotels and generally encourage those who can establish an economic base less exposed to circumstances beyond the community's control and understanding. The same story applies to Sudbury and Nanaimo. In Cape Breton, the New Dawn community development corporation is producing goods and services for the city of Sydney. People are increasingly not only working in the communities but for them as well. Economic and social lives are being drawn closer together.

What level of trade and outside exposure is right for a community? This question is difficult to answer. One of us has been engaged in an exercise in British Columbia, where members in economically depressed communities are being encouraged to sit down together and participate in an examination of their communities' export and import structure. The other recently conducted a similar exercise in the Inuit communities of Northern Labrador in which the current importance and future potential of local resource harvesting and processing were examined.[6] At the very least, communities should be aware of their degree of dependency and vulnerability, and also that over time they can alter the balance and assume a greater degree of control.

What is true for nations and communities also applies to households. As we have indicated earlier, households have increasingly become deskilled by specializing (at first, generally by the male household member, but increasingly by a second adult household member) in a narrow range of commercially marketable skills.   Essentially, households are trading (exporting) their marketable skills to outsiders (employers) in exchange for wages and the goods and services (imports) this income purchases.   But just as nations and communities do, households lose control over their ability to provide for themselves because they have little control over their exports (wage income).   And without the income from their exports, they run unfavorable trade balances, initially going into debt and finally subsisting on whatever aid they can obtain from government and extended family sources. When household members become unemployed and bankrupt, and because they have lost many of their survival or life-skills, they are unable to produce much for themselves--just as are import-dependent nations and communities when uncontrolled outside factors quickly change.

Undoubtedly, most households today have very high exposure levels to outside forces (which is frequently referred to as the high interdependency of modern urbanized households).   While a nation that obtains 50 percent of its goods and services through exchanges with people abroad is a rarity, it is likely that most households--certainly urban ones--are subject to this level of exposure at an even higher rate.   As long as outside factors do not change, households do not question their high level of outside exposure because it is the price they seem willing to pay for a high and growing level of material prosperity.

Outside factors have changed for a considerable number of Canadian households in the past few years, however, and an increasing number are asking how they became so vulnerable. They are now looking for ways of gaining more control over their lives, even if it means a reduced basket of material goods. Community-based, informal economic activities are one method to obtain greater control.

Now contrast this with the strategy for economic renewal that is urged upon us by most economists and most governments. With minor variations, it consists of the following elements:

(i)   Greater dependence on "free markets" and free trade for the provision of a growing proportion of society's goods and services.

(ii)   These markets and trade should be increasingly universal in scope and instantaneous in operation--hence, local markets should be displaced by national and international ones.

(iii)   It follows that there should be a greater international division of labor, more specialization and more dependence on long-distance trade for a greater variety of goods and even services.

(iv) To meet these objectives, Canada's particular strategy should be to develop its natural resources for export, to attempt to develop world class excellence in such limited areas as transportation and communications technology and, where this is not possible, to climb aboard as junior partner in such areas as aerospace and defense research and production.

(v) It follows that the maintenance of local, regional or even national production capabilities for essentially domestic purposes is counterproductive, because if we are successful in specialization and export, we can buy all of those things more cheaply than we can make them.

(vi) To succeed in this strategy, we must be ruthless in letting industries producing for domestic purposes wither and die, and we must encourage people to move to where the new jobs will be.

How can a viable informal economy be sustained in the context of this strategy? Clearly, it would be very difficult. If people are to uproot themselves and their families to roam about the country in search of new jobs every few years, then the family and community basis of the informal economy is severely jeopardized. To a limited degree, a country such as Canada will always have to depend on the willingness of a small proportion of the labor force to relocate, often at isolated frontier locations. But recent suggestions by small business representatives (for example, that the social security net in Canada is an impediment to small business because it reduces geographic mobility) seem less tenable to us. Small business does not, for the most part, operate in an international market. If small enterprise is to serve local needs, surely it has a responsibility to enhance, rather than diminish, the stability of local communities.

The cost of economic solutions like the massive retooling of society or constant migration in search of jobs--which is what high tech and megaproject solutions call for--is the continued uprooting of the family and community fabric which enables us to meet at least part of our economic needs by informal means. In formal economic calculations, labor is simply a commodity to be moved about so as to achieve maximum efficiency. No economic value is placed on the social fabric, and thus no cost is attributed to tearing it apart, which is seen as purely a "social" problem. The result is the need to replace--sometimes at great complexity and cost and in a formal way--the means by which people in small familiar groups routinely and informally did many things for themselves.

Similarly, if local markets are to be progressively replaced by international ones, a greater variety of distinctive local needs will be met with international standardized products, at the expense of viable local producers and products. While international specialization makes a lot of sense for highly complex and innovative products like commercial aircraft and computers, it makes much less sense for simple daily needs like food, small appliances and entertainment. Just as competent and self-reliant individuals or households can take care of at least a moderate range of their own needs, so communities, regions or nations that seek to be free and independent must also be competent to take care of their basic needs.

Conclusion: The Politics of Small Scale

The traditional political spectrum goes from left to right, but in recent years as the number and type of public issues grow, it has become increasingly difficult to place issues on this traditional spectrum without creating inconsistencies. When it comes to categorizing economic issues, the left traditionally favors nationalization, lots of government and greater redistribution of rewards. The right favors free enterprise, little or no government intervention, commercial profit motives and little redistribution of rewards. The latter claims to represent the individual against the system.

One of the difficulties that the notion of informal economic activity faces in gaining political acceptance is that it does not fit well on this traditional left-right political spectrum: it is neither socialist, liberal or conservative. None of the traditional labels stick. Undoubtedly, this inability to associate informal activity with any traditional political party or ideology makes it difficult for people who evaluate ideas, policies and events in traditional political terms for purposes of accepting and understanding new ideas. A certain amount of confusion arises: socialists and liberals attracted to some of the ideas feel they unwittingly may be embracing conservative ideals; at the same time, conservatives wanting to adopt some of the new approaches fear they may be endorsing collectivist principles.

There are several reasons for this confusion. In the first instance, informal economic activities and local economic development depend on individual, household and neighborhood initiative and enterprise. The words local, initiative and enterprise generally evoke thoughts of local boards of trade and free enterprise. But there is also a need for collective action and mutual aid, which are traditionally liberal and socialist ideas. Moreover, collective community support here does not imply a big government bent on nationalizing informal enterprises or developing complicated and inflexible programs to manage and control them from a distance. These approaches have come to be identified in recent years with liberal governments, but our approach rejects massive government intervention. Hence, it may appear to some to be a conservative idea. But conservatives who warm to the sound of local enterprise seldom warm to the idea of collective control: not only does it suggest big government but also an intrusion in the rights of management and an interference with free market decision-making processes.

There may also be confusion over our characterization of formal and informal activity along big-small lines. A small businessperson driven by the commercial profit motive has many business interests in common with small collectives and co-ops and briarpatch enterprises. This is so even though the small businessperson is uncomfortable with the fact that these other groups are often motivated by social objectives and frequently conduct their enterprises in non-conventional, collectivist ways. But ambivalent feelings are also held by some small businesspeople towards big commercial businesses. Big and small businesses are motivated by the same commercial forces; the people who run them all feel like "businesspeople" who, in many cases, share similar outlooks on life. But the small businessperson also knows that big businesses do not have the same concern as small businesses and, moreover, become big by driving out smaller businesses--often at least partly due to government regulation and financial assistance.

Similarly, members of small co-ops can frequently be heard complaining about large credit unions that have grown beyond their original ideals and are insensitive to the credit needs of small co-ops. In this sense, the smaller co-ops identify with many of the cash flow and credit problems of small businesspeople--and would want to coalesce with them on certain economic and local government issues, even though the two groups are most likely miles apart on the left-right political spectrum in terms of social issues. Since "small" does not easily follow left-right lines, our informal economy approach (which strongly favors small structures) should appeal to many people all along the left-right political spectrum.

The easy political acceptance of more informal activity along traditional party lines is also confounded by attitudes towards sexual equality and feminism. Betty Friedan during a 1982 Ottawa seminar, sponsored by the Vanier Institute of the Family, stated, "We have come as far as we can come based on masculine structures. We now need more 'second-stage' structures." Second-stage structures are those that respect a wider variety of individual and family needs in the economy and which permit a much greater sharing of household, community and labor force tasks and rewards. Formal economic structures are perceived as more masculine, while informal structures are more feminine. We saw this in our discussion of the nature of formal and informal activity. As a consequence, far-right conservatives who may feel favorably towards informal activity because it represents small, individual and local initiative may, on the other hand, feel uncomfortable with it as they are traditionally suspicious of feminism and sexual equality--the household is a wonderful place to work, but not for men. And on the other end of the spectrum, there will be liberals and socialists who are uneasy with the informal economy since it does not represent nationalization and industrial organization, but nonetheless are attracted to it because it accords with their feminist values.

There are undoubtedly other crosscurrents that confuse people's political feelings about our approach. Appealing to the old left-right political spectrum is not likely to help identify allies among the many new and strange bedfellows, emerging in support of a shift towards informal economic activity. In our view, the essence of the informal economy is a democratic collective involvement, where decision making in economic organizations is directly responsible to the households and communities that support them and depend on them. Let the alliances form where they may.

APPENDIX A

HOW ECONOMISTS VIEW ECONOMIC
LIFE: PAST AND PRESENT

In the current textbook view of the world, economic life is quite simple and one dimensional. Firms act to maximize their profits, while households maximize their utilities. These are the two major groups of actors with quite limited and well-defined objectives. To realize profits requires the firm to pay constant attention to technical matters--decisions concerning the ratio of labor and capital employed, the type and level of technology used, the types and wages of employment for women and the disabled, the physical conditions of work, whether production is centrally or locally based and controlled. All of these decisions are made on the basis of how they affect commercial profit, not out of direct consideration over the quality of life of workers and their families. There is no social accounting.

The consumer, by the same token, operates on the premise of the "economic man"--the acquisitive animal whose wants can never be satiated, the individualistic competitor in the market-place relentlessly pursuing his own self-interest, the poker player in the zero-sum game. A fundamental principle of the market is that people get what they demand. The marketplace is pictured as a big financial democracy, where people vote for goods and services with dollar bills. But they forget that it is not a system which encourages a one-person/one-vote balloting system.

In all of this, one might well ask, where are the institutions of family and community? To the extent that we can equate family with household, current economics texts suggest that the role of the household in modern industrial society is limited to selling its factors of production to larger economic organizations

131

(firms) and purchasing the goods and services these organizations produce. The factor that households have to sell in the greatest abundance is labor, although some may also loan their savings or inheritances, or rent out their real property. This is clearly reflected in the composition of personal income in Canada. In 1980, for example, 76 percent was from wages and salaries (the return to labor) and this did not include the labor income of proprietors of unincorporated businesses and farms.

The conventional definition of "economic" today excludes the recognition and study of most household and other informal productive activity. Economists have developed a definition of economic activity that coincides with the empirical measure known as Gross National Product (GNP), and having done so pay little attention to activity outside the formal sector.

An easy way to determine whether today's mainstream economists are emphasizing the productive role played by households and community in their studies, and what would-be economists are being exposed to, is to consult introductory economics textbooks. While textbooks do not reflect the entire range of current economic thinking or the most recent trends, textbook material is generally based on the perceived doctrines and principles accepted by the majority (mainstream) of the profession. Most mainstream textbooks are similar in content and design, so choosing almost any widely adopted text yields a good indication of what economists mean by the term "economy."

The most influential economics textbook during the postwar period is that written by the U.S. Nobel Laureate Paul Samuelson.[1] In a recent Canadian version of his book, there is not a single reference to household or family in the detailed 20-page index. There is a six-paragraph discussion of cooperative enterprises and reference to Yugoslavian workers' cooperatives. Otherwise, the entire 950-page book is devoted to the problems of understanding the market economy with various degrees of government and institutional interventions ("imperfections"), such as trade unions and minimum wages.

The second text adapted for Canadian use looks slightly more promising from the index, but is not.[2] It too has a short discussion of cooperatives (simply as a legal form of business) and a two-page reference to the household. But even in these two pages the household is given perfunctory treatment, being acknowledged foremost as the consumer of the economy's output and less importantly as the ultimate owner of its resources. It briefly mentions the existence of certain household businesses (such as corner grocery stores and family farms), but the productive activity that goes on daily within Canadian households is not considered worthy of study by economists. In neither text is there an analysis of what, how or how much economic activity in the informal sector is carried on, or who performs it or for whom. The conventional wisdom, then, is that production is performed by firms and not households. The household's economic function is a passive one--to consume the output of firms.

Economies are seen as national units and are conventionally compared on that basis. We are all familiar with United Nations or OECD statistics which rank national economies according to per capita income, productivity, inflation, balance of payments and so forth. It is true that regional accounts are also prepared within nations, but these regions are defined as mere administrative districts. Examination of the economic functioning of "true" human communities has traditionally been left to anthropologists and sociologists.

At the other end of the scale is the household. Economists tend to equate the household with the family, and ask no further about the actual relations among its members or how the household itself operates as an economic system. The economist is indifferent to the composition of the household, except insofar as it might affect consumer demand. Even when the household is also a firm, for example, an incorporated family farm or business, it is assumed that these functions are entirely separate. In theory, the household as firm sells all of what it produces in the market, and the household as family buys all that it needs in the market.

There is no correspondence between economic and social institutions at the intermediate level of human organization, however. The firm is an economic institution with highly distinctive economic goals, and very often consists of perfect strangers welded together by authority and reward systems for specific ends. It is not at all the same as the community. For whether the community consists of a neighborhood or locality, or a group of likeminded people, its members know one another face-to-face as people, not simply as job incumbents. Neither economics as a field of study, nor any of the indicators of "the economy" about which we hear so much, tell us anything about the economic activity of the neighborhood, the village, the small group or of family and kin.

Of Times Past and Informal Economic Activity

Studying only formal economic activities in such a narrow textbook fashion is a fairly recent phenomenon among mainstream economists if earlier economic texts can be used as a guideline. Richard Ely in *An Introduction to Political Economy*, published in 1893, observed:

> A large part of production even now is household production, as it may be called, and is not designed for the market-place, which indeed takes no note of it. Every well-established household is an establishment where valuable things or quantities of utility are produced.[3]

And in a section headed "Misleading Comparisons between the Past and the Present," Ely concluded:

> Production of things which are bought and sold in the market-place, and are consequently readily estimated in money, is constantly gaining in importance on household production of material good things. Hence annual production of economic goods which we estimate in money, increases more rapidly than real annual production; and there is consequently, a tendency always to exaggerate progress, and, indeed, to count as progress some things which are retrogressive.[4]

Throughout Ely's text are references to economic science as the study of the economic activities of all of society's individuals. But even at the time he was writing, the relative decline of household-produced goods and the growth of the industrial sector made it inevitable that economists would progressively concentrate their attention on the industrialized economy and exclude informal economic activity.

Even by 1913, Professor Taussig in his *Principles of Economics* did not elaborate so fullsomely on the informal or household economy. The time had come instead to more fully explain the principles of the industrial economy of the U.S. due to the transformation of the whole economy as the exchange sector rapidly grew. Explanation was needed of the new principles governing the division of labor, the distribution of income, the role of the public sector and of taxes, the function and regulation of money and so on. Many of these decisions were formerly reached by different sets of household and community principles which were quite unlike the principles being introduced by the growing exchange economy.

Nonetheless, as to what constituted "productive" labor, Taussig was quite clear:

> We conclude, then, that all those whose labors satisfy wants --all those who bring about satisfaction or utilities--are to be reckoned as taking part in production, and are to be called productive laborers. Certain it is, whatever phraseology we care to apply, that no conclusions of importance for economics flow from the distinction between those who shape material wealth and those who bring about utilities of other kinds.[5]

Would the majority of mainstream economists today fully or forcefully endorse such a statement?

Of considerable interest is Taussig's colorful and detailed chapter on cooperative enterprises run by workers.[6] Unlike later textbook writers, he did not just briefly discuss cooperatives as simply a narrow organizational form of business. Rather, he examined the principles and likely outcomes of a cooperative movement as an alternative to capitalism. His discussion was contained under enticing headings such as: "Cooperative Attempts to Dispense with the Businessman"; "Cooperation in Production Would Most Affect the Social Structure"; "Causes of Failure, the Rarity of the Business Qualities and the Limitations of Workingmen." While Taussig presented a balanced review of the principles and workings of cooperatives, he did not feel that the movement would make much progress in a North America dedicated to free enteprise.

A contemporary of Taussig at Harvard University, Sumner Slichter, who authored the text *Modern Economic Society* in 1931, clearly spelled out why economics was becoming a study of the industrial economy:

> Most of us produce very little for our own consumption but sell our labor or the products of our labor and, with the money thus obtained, buy what we desire. This means that buying and selling are far more important in modern economic life than at any time in the past ... our study of modern economic society must consist very largely of an inquiry into how buying and selling work under existing conditions, how prices are made....[7]

By 1931, mainstream economic texts were dealing extensively with the problems of industrialized exchange economies; nonetheless, there were explicit references to household production. Concern for the welfare of the household is perhaps best expressed by Slichter in a long chapter entitled "The Position of the Consumer." Here, the detrimental effects of advertising are prophetically and delightfully enumerated:

> Business enterprises invariably urge the consumer to buy, never not to buy. The custom of going without hats, for example, must make headway without support from the business world ... The money and skill of business are invariably devoted to persuading him to buy the new, regardless of whether or not he would gain more satisfaction by using the old a little longer ... For example, it is more profitable to stimulate a demand for newness rather than for durability, because, if consumers prefer durable things, the frequency with which each person can be sold will be diminished.[8]

And finally, for the household not as consumer but as producer, Slichter warned:

> The home industries lose out in competition with the factory because there is no one to say a word on their behalf. The Buffalo bakers recently began a cooperative advertising campaign to enlarge the cake market ... housewives still make about 80 percent of the sweet goods. But who is to finance a rebuttal in favor of home baking?[9]

The prevailing view in more recent times was, of course, different. Only 27 years later, during the period when the industrialized U.S. economy was at its peak, students reading the classic economics text by Paul Samuelson were treated to these words after a brief and cheerful discussion on the merits of advertising: "Only observe a young couple about to buy a high-fidelity phonograph set. Note their hours of careful study and field work. What Arabian master of the art of buying and selling can match their professional competence? What laboratory scientist, their meticulous zeal?"[10] In effect, advertising cannot alter our economic behavior.

During this same period when Slichter was proclaiming the virtues of household consumption and production, J.M. Clark, a noted Chicago economist, published an economics book that was to become a classic in mainstream economic theory, *The Economics of Overhead Costs*.[11] But even as a mainstream document there were frequent references to the applicability of its principles concerning fixed costs (overhead) to the operation of the household. Clark proposed that we examine how households (individually and collectively) could better "spread out" their overhead costs by doing things such as:

> ... buying, cooking, planning meals, etc. ... Indeed, one of our distinctive modern tasks is to bring into being a fund of really scientific information on these matters and to mobilize it for the service of the private household. ... [12]

Finally, mention must be repeated of an economics book (but not a mainstream textbook) published in 1934 by Margaret Reid, *Economics of Household Production.*[13] This book attempted to analyze the household economy in much the same way mainstream economists were analyzing and measuring formal economic activity. Reid viewed the household from a production perspective, which required it to make decisions concerning such things as the allocation of its members' time and resources and what should be produced at home and what bought in the market. Reid analyzed the factors influencing these decisions, in addition to making estimates of the type of household work performed, the value of it and those members who performed it. Reid's inquiry was launched by a concern similar to ours:

> The productive work of the household has been overlooked, even though more workers are engaged in it than any other single industry. The household is an integral part of our whole economic system. Only if it is viewed in this way can we become aware of the labor costs and productive activities necessary to maintain present standards of living. Unless this is done we cannot rightly appraise the economic role of homekeeping women ... The more we have concentrated on money values the more we have overlooked that part of our economic system which is not organized on a profit basis. [14]

Unfortunately for the study of economics (and home economics as well), Reid's contribution remained largely overlooked, and it is only recently that the household is again being examined from a production perspective.

Mention should also be made of a group of economists--often labeled the "institutionalists"--who fell in varying degrees outside of the mainstream of economics, but were precursors of a modern resurgence in the field of economic study. Most notable was

Thorstein Veblen who, writing at the turn of the century, coined the popular phrase "conspicuous consumption" and spent a lifetime criticizing American capitalism and the economists who often unwittingly defended it.[15] Much of what Veblen said 80 years ago is now being repeated by economists today, but with greater popularity and acceptance than in his time.

In summing up this earlier period of mainstream economic thinking, it becomes clear that during the period 1890-1940 the trend towards production outside the household and immediate community attracted the increasing descriptive and analytical attention of the day's mainstream economists. But in these earlier texts, there is still an appreciation of household production, as well as other forms of organizing the industrial sector. What is astonishing is how modern mainstream texts (covering roughly the post-World War II period to the present) can so quickly forget and ignore the household and community roots of the North American economy.

Between the end of World War II and the present, mainstream economics became increasingly preoccupied with studying the industrialized exchange economy. Economics no longer questioned the fundamentals or the desirability of a vast, highly interdependent system of market exchange based on private profit. There was no talk of the underlying philosophy, politics or derivation of private market exchange or of the distribution of labor or income. The commercial market system was studied as if it was always right and always there.

Most textbooks also did not do a good job of accurately studying what was there since they still portrayed the economy as being one primarily of craftspeople and shopkeepers, as described 200 years earlier by Adam Smith. Each individual was portrayed as controlling and being totally responsible for his (seldom her) economic destiny, even though by the 1900s there was considerable and ongoing centralization and concentration of economic control. The "invisible hand" of free market forces was rapidly giving way to the administration of commercial forces through the not so invisible hands of new and powerful interests. The day of big business, big labor and big government had arrived.

But mainstream economic studies increasingly turned inwards and enormous "technical" advancements were made, some highly useful but most of dubious value. Sophistication in itself, generally accomplished with the use of mathematics, became a major end of economic study and the appreciated currency, especially in academic circles. One could fairly sum up the 1940-

1980 period in economics as a time in which economists understood more and more about less and less.

Because the study of economics became very dry, technical and exclusive, it also became parochial and fragmented with little interest in the findings concerning society and human behavior coming out of studies in philosophy, history, politics, sociology and ecology. It is no wonder, therefore, that the pioneers of more fundamental approaches to economics, more "whole" approaches, should find eager and thirsty disciples today.

APPENDIX B

THE VILLAGE ECONOMY:
THE INFORMAL ECONOMY AS A WAY OF LIFE

To illustrate the workings of the informal economy more clearly, we use an example largely unfamiliar to most Canadians: the "village economy" of small Inuit and Indian communities in the North. A brief account of recent economic circumstances and changes in those communities highlights both the nature of informal economic activity itself and the impact of the expansion of formal activity upon it.[1]

An hour's walk around a modern Inuit community or northern Indian reserve does not immediately reveal much that differs from a rural village in southern Canada. They may be usually less prosperous, but there are no igloos or tepees or kayaks and only a few dog teams remain. Instead, there are likely to be rows of modest frame houses, snowmobiles and pickup trucks parked outside and TVs, freezers and sofas inside. Only the few pelts and carcasses hanging outside reveal another economy, which many policy makers and social scientists for years supposed would have disappeared by now in the wake of "modernization."

However, recent research in these communities across the North reveals a different reality. While Native northerners now spend more time at--and derive more income from--non-traditional pursuits than was so a generation ago, they continue to produce much of their own food and are in most areas essentially self-sufficient in protein. Virtually all of this food is either consumed by the household that produced it or distributed among other households on the basis of mutual aid and obligation. Jobs and wages are merely a part of the economic picture. They are not its sole basis, and few would like them to become such. The

141

economy of northern Native communities is no longer primitive or even pre-industrial, yet it continues to be very different from the dominant Canadian economy. Elements of pre-industrial or petty commodity production--self-employment, household production, non-market exchange--are combined with wage labor, transfer payments and small business in a pluralistic seasonal economy. Instead of a traditional economy being replaced by a "modern" one, there is now a distinctive "Native" or "village" economy, which shows many indications of perpetuating itself into the future.

There are thus two ways of life in northern Canada today, often referred to as two economies--the Native or village economy, on the one hand, and the industrial economy on the other. They are not completely analogous to the formal and informal economies as we have described them, partly because there is in the North a strong ethnic, cultural and institutional basis for distinguishing between the two forms of economic activity, which is not the case in southern Canada. To simplify the discussion, we describe the economies in their model or archetype form.

The industrial economy in the North typically consists of three sectors: government, corporate and resident small business. The government sector is much larger, proportionately, than is the case in metropolitan Canada, but relatively little of it is under direct local control. The corporate sector consists of large, externally controlled organizations which extract, process and export goods. The more isolated the locale and the more difficult the environment, the more sophisticated and capital-intensive is the corporate sector likely to be (and the larger and more influential its individual members are likely to be). The resident, small business sector mostly provides services, rather than producing goods.

The industrial economy is motivated chiefly by the search for staple resource exports on the part of metropolitan interests; it is organized by corporate enterprise and it is supported by the apparatus of the modern state. The mode of production is capitalist, and it is totally reliant on external support systems and productive factors--heavy infusions of capital, specialized man-agerial and labor skills and a complex infrastructure of transport, communications and administration. In its goods-producing sector, the industrial economy is capital-intensive, energy-intensive and technologically sophisticated, while its service and administrative sectors require less capital and technology but more labor. Money is the exclusive medium of exchange and prices are determined by "market forces" as these are commonly understood. Income is distributed unequally in the form of wages, salaries, profits, interest and rents, and the manner in which this income is spent, saved or reinvested in productive factors is unequally determined.

Frontier development needs people who are prepared to move from job to job and place to place, sometimes frequently and on short notice. A premium is placed on personal mobility. Ties of family and friends and the desire for a stable community life are at odds with the needs of industrial development in the North. Some large corporations attempt to minimize the consequences, for example, by improving living conditions outside the workplace, reducing labor turnover and providing transport to and communications with home. But these measures are inevitably viewed as costs of production and must be justified as such.

Under modern conditions, the village economy consists of two distinctive sectors: a subsistence or domestic sector and a commodity or exchange sector, plus the incorporation of elements of the productive economy. The subsistence sector produces goods for direct domestic consumption, while in the exchange sector goods are produced for trade, either for other goods or services or for cash. The basic unit of production and consumption in each is the household.

The village economy exploits a combination of readily available resources and opportunities primarily for local consumption and benefit. The economy is neither capital- nor energy-intensive, and relies on relatively small and simple productive factors which may be produced or purchased--and maintained--by the individual household. Money is one of several media of exchange, along with domestically produced goods. Within the domestic sphere, which accounts for a large part of economic activity, value is determined only partially by market forces with cultural and political considerations also playing an important role.

Income in the form of domestic produce is distributed in more or less egalitarian fashion amongst an extended group. Cash income derived from commodity exchange tends to accrue to the producer, but such means as sharing and gambling promote a rapid circulation and distribution of cash (and to some extent of the means of production) throughout the community. Savings are virtually non-existent, reinvestment decisions are made at the household level and there is a high propensity to spend cash income soon after its realization. The village economy in recent times has suffered a chronic shortage of cash. In its goods-producing sector, it is much more labor-intensive than the industrial economy.

For many Native northerners, a substantial amount of production, exchange and distribution still occurs through non-market mechanisms. Wants and needs are commonly expressed or recognized directly among individuals who are in more or less continuous contact with one another--and through custom and convention, rather than through an impersonal market. Much distribution is based on kinship, friendship, alliance, need or some convention other than purchasing power. Much exchange is based on generalized and balanced reciprocity, rather than on specific and quantified cash transactions.

It should not be surprising, then, that the values which traditional Indian and Inuit ideology reinforces include family solidarity, a sense of place and community, stability, tradition, egalitarianism, cooperation, non-assertiveness and conflict avoidance. Where the Native economy is strong, there is great emphasis on the socialization of children through traditional activities, on mutual aid and sharing and on a sense of stewardship of the basic natural resources available to the society. There is no private ownership of land or resources, although certain areas are by tradition used by certain groups, and there are socio-political means of allocating access to land and resources within the group and of controlling access by non-members.

Although it is useful for certain purposes to analyze the village and industrial economies separately, they are strongly interconnected. The sustained production of goods for exchange began with the fur trade. The most important feature of this exchange relationship for most northern Native peoples, however, was that the production of commodities for exchange was by no means completely incompatible with the continued production of essential goods for domestic use. Indeed, the fur trade was quite compatible with domestic production. The production of commodities for exchange did not require a major reorientation of the social or economic system. The domestic mode of production, although rendered dependent on trade relations with (and later, subsidies from) another, more powerful and sophisticated society, nonetheless remained both viable and dominant, in that with a minimum of reorganization it was capable of producing goods for both domestic consumption and commodity exchange.

When it was the predominant or sole economy in the North, one of the chief problems with this economy was the terms of trade in the exchange sector. So long as commodity prices were high, Native peoples had considerable purchasing power for goods and services not produced in the domestic sphere. They had no control over the terms of trade, however, and were therefore highly vulnerable to external economic changes. In the 1940s and 1950s, for example, the Native economy was in widespread crisis due to declining prices for the commodities it exported--chiefly furs--coupled with a rapid inflation in the cost of imported goods. This event along with others precipitated major changes in the relations between the Native and non-Native economies in the North.

During the third quarter of the 20th century, in line with new possibilities and perceptions of the northern frontier, federal, provincial and territorial administrations of all political persuasions adopted a more or less common approach to the socio-economic development of northern Native peoples. It was concluded that the traditional way of life was dying or dead and that the only avenue for Native peoples was to join the white man's world. The short-run solution to the problems of the day was the provision of health and welfare measures. The long-run solution was to educate Native peoples and give them wage employment, for only in this way could they be prepared for the industrialization of the North which surely lay ahead.

The rise of large-scale resource development activity and of large, modern government centers in the North made it seem that the two economies functioned independently. Although they were in geographic proximity, there were virtually no linkages between them in terms of cash or commodity flow, transport, labor or technology. The only apparent point of contact was in the small business or government sectors, located chiefly within the larger settlements. There, some Native peoples tended to be incorporated into the lowest levels of the occupational and wage structure (often on a casual basis) or into the ranks of the unemployed.

This apparent independence of the two sectors gave rise to the notion of the dual economy. It was correctly observed that economic growth (or measures to promote it) in the industrial sector generally failed to result in growth in the Native sector. It was incorrectly concluded, however, that the two sectors were therefore functionally independent; that the industrial economy was an enclave in which development took place, while the Native economy was stagnant and incapable of improvement. Policies based on this analysis involved moving people out of the traditional sector and into the modern one, where everyone would experience the benefits of development. This model of the northern economy was paralleled by theories of social change which saw a process of movement--physically, psychologically and ideologically--of Native peoples from one to the other, from traditional life on the land to wage labor in the settlements.

Despite the relative absence of direct linkages between them, the two economies not only were and are dependent on the metropolitan economies of the south but functionally related to them. The Native economy is by no means an aboriginal enclave, unaffected by the metropolitan economy; rather it is directly connected to it by virtue of its exchange component--these exchanges being, by and large, administered in the South but effected in the North. In all the economic statistics about employment and income, what had gone unnoticed was the existence of a substantial domestic economy, which provided a large part of local food requirements and a smaller proportion of clothing and fuel needs. If evaluated on a replacement basis, hunting, fishing, trapping and wooding contributed several thousands of dollars per household of income in kind each year (see Chapter Five).

More recent developments suggest, however, that even the absence of direct linkages between the two economies was, in fact, only a temporary stage. The advance of industrial development in the North has resulted in widespread conflict over land use, resource management and the allocation of public and private funds, as well as the concerted encouragement of Native peoples to join the industrial labor force. In short, direct competition has arisen between the two economies for the essential factors of production: land, labor and capital. Whatever inherent weaknesses the village economy is alleged to have, it is now apparent that its performance is not simply indifferent to the growth of the industrial economy. It is adversely affected by it, precisely because of the nature of the linkages between the two.

Just as the two modes of production are linked in the macroeconomic ways described above, they are also linked at the microeconomic level by individual participation. The terms "Native" and "industrial" do not, in fact, describe a strict ethnic separation of economic activity. While virtually all white residents of the North are largely or entirely dependent on the industrial economy, very few Native peoples are totally dependent on the traditional domestic and exchange sectors alone. Instead, because wages and transfer payments have become major sources of the cash which is so essential to the effective operation of the village economy, they rely on some mixture of the two.

A typical Native household in a small community has several streams of income--from wage employment, from trapping and handicraft production, from hunting and fishing and from transfer payments (such as family allowances or occasional social assistance). Since many of these activities are seasonal, each member of the household might be engaged in any one of them at any particular time. Income from each source may then be pooled for common use, rather than being appropriated privately by each member.

Not only are most household members contributing outside income; most also participate in the domestic economy of the household. Hunting and fishing have already been mentioned. Typically, however, such a household produces for itself a broad range of services which are frequently purchased outside the household in an urban industrial setting. Almost all meals are prepared and eaten at home, child care and housekeeping are internal responsibilities, and the household is also substantially self-sufficient in the maintenance and repair of productive equipment, home maintenance and renovation and, in the subarctic at least, in fuel wood.

Also significant in the village economy are the relations among households. These include partnerships or alliances in productive activity--trapping, hunting and fishing--as well as networks for the sharing of domestic goods and services. All of these streams of income and networks of production and distribution are combined in a long-range balance, each taken advantage of when the opportunity arises, and each being especially important at certain seasons or in certain years or at certain stages of one's life and in the developmental cycle of the household.

One of the problems with the Native economy is that of all the factors of production the one most usually deficient is capital, due to the difficulties of accumulating sufficient cash over an extended period. Very often, the returns from exchange production are insufficient to meet the capital requirements (operation and maintenance) of the entire complex of domestic and exchange production. That is why subsidies or wage employment have become important to the maintenance of traditional activities. People may have to take on seasonal, or even permanent employment, to finance their traditional activities as commodity exchange is less and less able to meet these needs. This was the real crisis of the fur trade a generation ago and why transfer payments came to play such a key role.

Because capital input requirements increase greatly, the problem of cash shortages becomes more acute as new and more sophisticated technology is employed in these activities. As well, the returns on traditional activities are almost never sufficient to generate the enormous surplus required to maintain the government and resident small business sectors which now typically exist in the North. Consequently, domestic and exchange production are often viewed as irrelevant, if not downright unproductive, by industrial society on the frontier.

All this leads to a second problem: the village economy is increasingly vulnerable to events and decisions beyond its knowledge and control. Commodity price instability, inflation, resource-management policies, environmental alteration or degradation, economic development and social welfare policies, technological innovations--all emanate from the dominant industrial economy and can have profound effects on the local one as well.

The greater the interaction between the two societies (or more particularly, the greater the penetration and influence of the dominant society), the more vulnerable the village economy becomes. As trade and movement increase between the two--not only of commodities but of labor and capital--the more the domestic sector of the Native economy is transformed by market forces and industrial imperatives and the more dependent Native communities and society become--and the less able to defend their own interests.

This raises many problems for those of the Native peoples who wish to retain the essentials of the village economy. Perhaps the most important one is the allocation of labor time, since the viability of that economy now depends on some combination of wage labor and subsidies. The time that individuals or households must allocate to the industrial economy may vary, depending on what seasonal or casual labor is available and how remunerative it is relative to commodity and domestic production. The characteristic pattern for much of the 20th century, and the chief factor that has enabled the village economy to survive in our time, has been that much less time has had to be allocated to wage labor than to domestic and exchange production.

What is clear in this situation is that wage income is not always a net addition to total income. In certain circumstances, it is obtained only at the expense of a certain portion of domestic income, so that the net benefits from wage employment are not necessarily as great as standard economic indicators might suggest. Indeed, for a variety of reasons, relating chiefly to the current system of personal taxation and individual transfer payments in Canada, losses in income from the traditional sector would have to be made up by substantially greater amounts of wage income to provide equivalent purchasing power, quite apart from social considerations. To the extent that Native peoples-- primarily oriented to traditional activities--desire wage employment, they seek casual or seasonal employment in which they can earn predetermined amounts of cash to meet specified needs, rather than full-time career-oriented employment.

One of the chief problems with wage employment is that it demands time. By comparison, the welfare system does not, which is why those oriented chiefly to domestic production find that essential cash resources are much more sensibly obtained from the welfare system than from wage employment. The entire range of social welfare benefits has assumed great importance in the Native economy within the last generation. These benefits include not only social assistance payments (which contrary to popular opinion account for only a small part of personal income in most northern Native communities) but also family allowances, old age pensions, child tax credits, unemployment insurance and payments under other similar programs. This impact on the Native economy has been as much incidental as intentional, however, since these payments are generated from national or provincial programs, which were neither conceived nor modified with Native peoples' interests in mind, even though the role of these payments in northern social and economic life is very different from that in urban industrial Canada. Consequently, the welfare state system has come to be seen by Native peoples as an economic resource to be tapped like any other. The advantage of the recently established Income Security Programme for the Quebec Cree, as a consequence of the James Bay and Northern Quebec agreement, is that it explicitly recognizes the issue of time allocation between the two economies, and is specifically designed to meet Cree needs (except perhaps in its bureaucratic administration as a state program).

The continuing existence and viability of the village economy goes far to explain why Native peoples have been more and more emphatically asserting their present reliance on the land and their desire for such reliance to continue. It also is one of the reasons why they do not always find it in their interest to accept the wage employment opportunities which governments have so assiduously promoted for them.

The main problem with massive industrial development, as seen by many Native northerners, was that it would destroy the balance and security of their social and economic life. Certainly, they relied on wage employment, but often as an addition to--rather than a substitute for--the alternative means of making a living. Many families have already found out that if everyone in the household worked for wages with no one hunting any more, their grocery bills skyrocketed, they were not eating as well and life was not as enjoyable. So the prospect of these massive developments cutting off or making less viable the variety of income and activity streams to which the people had access--as well as reducing the availability of fish and wildlife through environmental damage--was very alarming. Many families were also discovering that some of the high wages paid to an individual working away from the community tended to be spent outside the community so that no real benefit accrued to the household and the community.

Native peoples do not see the issue as a stark choice between a high-tech, urban industrial future, on the one hand, and returning to a romantic bucolic past on the other. Instead, the issue is to find the right balance between formal and informal activities--between wage employment and the money economy, or a domestic and community economy (with its strong emphasis on mutual aid and sharing, family and community life, and traditional institutions, such as the collective land tenure system). Consequently, in the process of assessing the impacts of large-scale development activity in the North, there has been a substantial shift from a focus on the purely economic welfare of individuals to one of the social welfare of whole communities.

Another part of Canada where this kind of economy is identifiable and has been well documented is in rural Newfoundland.[2] In the outports, many families have routinely produced much of their own food by fishing, hunting and gardening, their own firewood for home heating and their own lumber for houses and boats. Many families erect their own houses, fishracks and wharves on plots handed down over generations. Households can count on one another for aid when in need and neighborly cooperation and exchange are part of the system. Both self-sufficiency and mutual aid continue to be a part of everyday life, along with wage labor, transfer payments, small business and new technologies.

While there is little documentation of the village economy outside of Newfoundland and the North, in all probability it exists to some degree throughout rural Canada wherever land holdings and productive investments are small and dispersed, the population is relatively stable and where primary production has not become heavily specialized and industrialized.

In its more obvious form, however, it is not only dependent on the principles of mutual aid and self-sufficiency but on the effective use of and control over natural resources and the lands and waters that sustain them. That is why small, resource-based communities in all parts of Canada have so often resisted the competitive use of their land or water base for industrial development, despite the apparent attraction of the jobs so created.

By these criteria, one would therefore expect to find significant amounts of informal production and exchange in the Maritimes, the lower St. Lawrence, western Quebec, eastern and northern Ontario, the northern fringe of the Prairies and in some of the interior valleys and small coastal settlements of British Columbia. Such economic activity would be much less significant in those parts of the Prairies and in southern Ontario and Quebec where there are large and intensive livestock, grain and vegetable farms.

What is significant about the village economy is that although it has greatly changed from the somewhat romanticized and antiquated view that many Canadians have of it, it has not disappeared. Instead, it has demonstrated remarkable staying power in the face of all predictions, hopeful and otherwise, that it would be "modernized" out of existence.

Nonetheless, village economies have experienced substantial difficulties and tensions, at once seemingly resisting and yet being attracted to the expansion of the formal economy.

Studies of economic development and social change--especially of the agricultural and fisheries sectors, Indian and Inuit communities and ethnic and immigrant groups in Canada--generally show that with widespread industrial employment, household production tends to decline as a proportion of total production. Households must obtain a greater proportion of their needs through market exchange, rather than domestic production. This occurs in two ways: first, there is a tendency to specialize in commodity production for market exchange at the expense of domestic production and, secondly, there is a tendency to exchange labor power for cash and abandon household production altogether. As well, both persons and households become less interdependent economically. Mutual aid and sharing networks atrophy. Income, especially cash income, is viewed more as an individual posession and is less likely to be pooled on a household basis. As households become more isolated, differences among their income levels and well-being grow.

As personal and household incomes rise in an absolute sense, so does vulnerability to uncontrollable social forces at the local level, although the latter tendency is less easily and rapidly recognized (or celebrated) than the former. When wage employment becomes the dominant, nearly exclusive means by which the average household derives its income, its members must adopt appropriate attitudes and disciplines with respect to participation in the labor force, as well as the earlier described new patterns of expenditure and consumption.

People must now commit themselves to a long and costly education process for their children, largely outside their control. This is partly because their own skills are perceived to be of very limited value to the next generation. Emphasis shifts from learning a trade--a means of participating in the labor force from time to time when necessary or desirable--to planning a career. A career requires total and constant commitment to the formal economy--a calculated trajectory over a lifetime of investment and return on human capital. All other productive skills atrophy and time not devoted to one's career becomes leisure. Income is devoted to purchasing subsistence and enhancing leisure, neither of which is any longer possible without money.

The greater the reliance on wage and salary income, however, the greater is the need for formal institutional arrangements--both public and private--for long-term security and risk spreading, and the greater one's liability to all forms of taxation. With the decline of social solidarity at the level of kin and community, people must avert the risk of household economic catastrophe by investing in pensions, insurance and securities. Security is increasingly seen to depend on things and institutions, rather than people.

All of these trends require continuing financial obligations on a regular basis: monthly payments on mortgages, loans, consumer finance, pension plans, payroll deductions for welfare state programs and the like. These obligations are, of course, quite at odds with the dominant patterns of the informal economy--seasonal activity, irregular income and income in kind --in which households meet much of their daily subsistence needs by domestic production.

As these trends gather strength, the danger arises that the viability of the village or informal economy will be weakened. People will be less able to fall back on this economy in times of need both because the resources on which it relies are less available and because the skills, institutions and values it nurtures have atrophied.[3]

NOTES

CHAPTER ONE
PREVAILING CONSERVATIVE NOSTRUMS

1. George Gilder, *Wealth and Poverty* (New York: Basic Books, 1980).

2. David Crane, ed., *Beyond the Monetarists: Post-Keynesian Alternatives* (Toronto: James Lorimer & Co. for the Canadian Institute for Economic Policy, 1981).

3. J.K. Galbraith, *American Capitalism* (Boston: Houghton Mifflin Co., 1952) and *The New Industrial State* (Boston: Houghton Mifflin Co., 1967).

4. David P. Ross, *The Canadian Fact Book on Income Distribution* (Ottawa: Canadian Council on Social Development, 1980).

5. Milton Friedman, *Capitalism and Freedom* (Chicago: University of Chicago Press, 1962), Chapter XII.

6. OECD, *Past and Present Trends of Industrial Investment* (Paris: OECD, 1978).

7. Lester Thurow, *The Zero-Sum Society: Distribution and the Possibility for Economic Change* (New York: Basic Books, 1980).

8. Walter Anderson, ed., *Rethinking Liberalism* (New York: Avon Books, 1983); Abraham Rotstein, *Rebuilding From*

NOTES - CHAPTER ONE (continued)

Within (Toronto: James Lorimer & Co., 1984), Chapter 5; George Grant, *Technology and Empire: Perspectives on North America* (Toronto: University of Toronto Press, 1969); Martin Carnoy and Derek Shearer, *Economic Democracy* (New York: M.E. Sharpe, 1980); George McRobie, *Small is Possible* (New York: Harper & Row, 1981); and Murray Bookchin, *The Ecology of Freedom* (Palo Alto: Cheshire Books, 1982).

9.   Gregory Baum and Duncan Cameron, *Ethics and Economics: Canada's Catholic Bishops on the Economic Crisis* (Toronto: James Lorimer & Co., 1984).

CHAPTER THREE
THE NATURE OF INFORMAL ECONOMIC ACTIVITY

1.   For an early use of the term 'informal' to describe certain economic activity in the Third World, see Robert S. McNamara, *Address to the Board of Governors of the World Bank* (Washington: World Bank, September 1975). For a more technical example, see C.O. Moser, "Informal Sector or Petty Commodity Production: Dualism or Dependence in Urban Development?," *World Development* 6 (1978): 1041-1064.

2.   L.A. Johnson, "Independent Commodity Production: Mode of Production or Capitalist Class Formation?," *Studies in Political Economy* 6 (1981): 93-112.

3.   For some case examples, see W.M. Nicholls and W.A. Dyson, *The Informal Economy* (Ottawa: Vanier Institute of the Family, 1983).

4.   The views and values of the "back to the land movement" may be readily discerned from the pages of the Canadian

NOTES - CHAPTER THREE (continued)

journal *Harrowsmith* and the American journal *Countryside.*

5. E.F. Schumacher, *Small is Beautiful* (New York: Harper & Row, 1975).

6. L.C. Johnson, *The Seam Allowance: Industrial Home Sewing in Canada* (Toronto: Women's Educational Press, 1982).

7. Proceedings of a VIF Seminar, *Exploring Work and Income Opportunities in the 1980's: Our Future in the Informal Economy,* Fort Qu'Appelle, Saskatchewan, 1979 (Ottawa: Vanier Institute of the Family, 1979).

8. See, for example, the chapter, "Property and Proletarianization: Transformation of Simple Commodity Production in Canadian Farming and Fishing" in Wallace Clement, *Class, Power and Property* (Toronto: Methuen, 1983), pp. 225-243; and M. Hedley, "Reproduction and Evolving Patterns of Cooperation and Resource Transfer Among Domestic Producers," *Canadian Journal of Anthropology* 1 (1980): 141-147.

9. J.K. Galbraith argues that they are forced to do these things in order to survive in the same environment as large corporations, or what he calls the "planning system." See "Self-exploitation and Exploitation," Chapter 8 in *Economics and the Public Purpose* (Boston: Houghton Mifflin Co., 1973). While this is so, the fact that many people work very hard to become smallholders, and fiercely resist being forced out of smallholding once in, suggests that in their minds the rewards outweigh whatever income and security they have foregone in wage and salary employment.

10. See, for example, J. Chevalier, "There Is Nothing Simple About Simple Commodity Production," *Studies in Political Economy* 7 (1982): 89-124.

11. The Census of Agriculture does not record off-farm income by members of the farm family, other than the farmer himself.

NOTES - CHAPTER THREE (continued)

12. R. Bollman and A.D. Steeves, "The Stocks and Flows of Canadian Census Farm Operators, 1966-76," *Canadian Review of Sociology and Anthopology* 19 (1982): 576-590.

CHAPTER FOUR
THE STRUCTURES OF FORMAL AND
INFORMAL ECONOMIC ACTIVITY

1. J.K. Galbraith, *Economics and the Public Purpose* (Boston: Houghton Mifflin Co., 1973), Part 3.

2. Rein Peterson, *Small Business: Building a Balanced Economy* (Erin, Ont.: Press Porcepic, 1977).

3. For a brief historical description of New Dawn, see John Hanratty, *The New Dawn Story* (Ottawa: Health and Welfare Canada, 1981). National Council of Welfare's *Working Together* (Ottawa, 1978) discusses New Dawn and similar enterprises; and Susan Wismer and David Pell's *Community Profit* (Toronto: Is Five Press, 1981) deals more extensively with community economic development in general. The report of the departmental task force set up by Employment and Immigration Canada also discusses the importance of community job-creation efforts. (See *Labour Market Development in the 1980's* [Ottawa, 1981], Chapter 8.)

4. Hanratty, *New Dawn Story,* p. 11.

5. Ibid., p. 13.

6. S. Burns, *Home Inc.* (Garden City: Doubleday & Co., 1975); and J. Gershuny, *After Industrial Society? The Emerging Self-Service Economy* (London: MacMillan & Co., 1978).

NOTES - CHAPTER FOUR (continued)

7.   Margaret Reid, *Economics of Household Production* (New York: John Wiley & Sons, 1934), p. 11.

CHAPTER FIVE
MEASURING INFORMAL ECONOMIC ACTIVITY

1.   *Small Business in Canada* (Ottawa: Small Business Secretariat, Department of Industry, Trade and Commerce, 1984). The definitions and data in the following sections come from this publication.

2.   Statistics Canada, *Manufacturing Industries of Canada: National and Provincial Areas, 1978* (Ottawa: Supply and Services Canada, 1980); idem., *Type of Organization and Size of Establishments, 1970* (Ottawa, 1973); and idem., *Type of Ownership and Size of Establishments Engaged in Manufacturing in Canada, 1960* (Ottawa, 1962).

3.   Co-operative Union of Canada, *Co-operatives Canada '83* (Ottawa: CUC, 1983).

4.   Statistics Canada, *Financial Survey of Registered Charities, 1980* (Ottawa: Supply and Services Canada, 1983).

5.   David P. Ross, *Some Financial and Economic Dimensions of Registered Charities and Volunteer Activity in Canada* (Ottawa: Secretary of State, 1983).

6.   Statistics Canada, "An Overview of Volunteer Activity in Canada," Appendix in *Labour Force Survey* (May 1981).

7.   Ross, *Some Financial.*

8.   The sources for Table 2 are as follows: Labrador - P.J. Usher, *Renewable Resources in the Future of Northern*

NOTES - CHAPTER FIVE (continued)

Labrador (Nain: Labrador Inuit Association, 1982); Northern Quebec and James Bay - James Bay and Northern Quebec Native Harvesting Research Committee, various unpublished reports (Montreal, n.d.); Saskatchewan - P. Ballantyne et al., *Aski-Puko (The Land Alone)*, n.p., n.d.; British Columbia - H. Brody, *Maps and Dreams* (Vancouver: Douglas & McIntyre, 1981); Yukon - P. Dimitrov and M. Weinstein, *So That the Future Will Be Ours* (Ross River: Ross River Indian Band, 1984): Mackenzie Valley/Beaufort Sea - T.R. Berger, *Northern Frontier--Northern Homeland* (Report of the Mackenzie Valley Pipeline Inquiry), vol. 2 (Ottawa: Supply and Services Canada, 1977), Chapter 2, "Renewable Resources"; Baker Lake - Interdisciplinary Systems Ltd., *Effects of Exploration and Development in the Baker Lake Area* (Winnipeg, 1978): Pond Inlet - E. Treude (trans. by W. Barr), "Pond Inlet, Northern Baffin Island: The Structure of an Eskimo Resource Area," *Polar Geography* 6 (1977): 95-122.

9. Berger, *Northern Frontier*, vol. 2.

10. P.J. Usher, "Evaluating Country Food in the Northern Native Economy," *Arctic* 29 (1976): 105-120. See also above in note 8--Ballantyne; Berger; Interdisciplinary Systems; and Usher.

11. Berger, *Northern Frontier*, vol. 2.

12. Usher, *Renewable Resources*.

13. Statistics Canada, *Income Distributions by Size in Canada, 1981* (Ottawa: Supply and Services Canada, 1983).

14. The data in the following two paragraphs are taken from two background papers prepared for the Economic Council of Canada in 1980 by D. Wells, "Unrecorded Income in Rural Newfoundland," and P.M. Reid, "From Bays to Peninsulas." See also O. Brox, *Maintenance of Economic Dualism in Newfoundland* (St. John's: Institute for Social and Economic Research, Memorial University of Newfoundland, 1969); and A.P. Dyke, "Subsistence Production in the Houseland Economy of Rural Newfoundland" (St. Johns, 1968).

NOTES - CHAPTER FIVE (continued)

15.   The impact of industrial development on the village eco-
        nomy was a central issue in public inquiries concerning the
        Mackenzie Valley pipeline, the Alaska Highway pipeline and
        the Churchill River hydro electric project, as well as in
        injunctions sought by Native communities with respect to
        the James Bay hydro electric project and uranium mining in
        the central Keewatin District.

16.   P. Freundlich, C. Collins and M. Wenig, eds., *A Guide to
        Cooperative Alternatives* (New Haven: Community Publi-
        cations Cooperative, 1979).

17.   Statistics Canada, *Income Distributions by Size*, pp. 108-111.
        All following information concerning the economics of
        households is drawn from these pages.

18.   Sylvia Wargon, *Canadian Households and Families* (Ottawa:
        Supply and Services Canada, 1979), p. 51.   The historical
        data used in the discussion also come from this volume.

19.   D.H. Elliot, A.S. Harvey and D. Procos, "An Overview of the
        Halifax Time-Budget Study" (Halifax: Institute of Public
        Affairs, Dalhousie University, October 1973), p. 16.

20.   Kathryn Walker, "Household Work Time: Its Implication for
        Family Decisions," *Journal of Home Economics* 65, no. 7
        (October 1973): 7-11.

21.   Martha F. Hill, "Investments of Time in Houses and
        Durables," Chapter 9 in Thomas E. Juster and Frank P.
        Stafford, eds., *Time, Goods and Well-Being* (Ann Arbor:
        Institute for Social Research, University of Michigan,
        1985).

22.   Meg Luxton, *More than a Labour of Love* (Toronto: Wo-
        men's Educational Press, 1980).   This book provides an
        interesting account of how three generations of Canadian
        women see their role as homemakers and whether their
        domestic work is easier today than in the past. In general,
        the answer seems to be no.

NOTES - CHAPTER FIVE (continued)

23. John Robinson, *Changes in American's Use of Time: 1965-1975* (Cleveland: Communication Research Center, Cleveland State University, August 1977).

24. The results of this study are summarized in Joann Vanek, "Time Spent in Housework," *Scientific American* (November 1974): 116-120.

25. J. Gershuny and G. Thomas, "A Study of Changing Time-Use Patterns, Britain 1961-1974," preliminary manuscript, 1981.

26. M. Lutz and K. Lux, *The Challenge of Humanistic Economics* (Menlo Park, Calif.: Benjamin-Cummings Publishing Co., 1979). This book contains an excellent critique of the mainstream economists' practice of assuming that human needs are interchangeable and thus capable of being fulfilled through an exchange process. See especially Chapter 1.

27. Hill, "Investments of Time"; and H.J. Adler and O. Hawrylyshyn, "Estimates of the Value of Household Work in Canada, 1961 and 1971," in *Review of Income and Wealth* (Ottawa: Supply and Services Canada for Statistics Canada, 1978). These studies contain good reviews of the different methods used for evaluating the economic value of household activity.

28. Adler and Hawrylyshyn, "Estimates of the Value," p. 338.

29. The Proulx study is cited in S.J. Wilson, *Women, the Family and the Economy* (Toronto: McGraw-Hill Ryerson, 1982), p. 62. See also Wilson's review of the results of other partial studies, pp. 59-62.

30. W. Gauger and K. Walker, "Household Work: Can We Add It to G.N.P.?," *Journal of Home Economics* 65, no. 7 (October 1973): 12-15.

31. Hill, "Investments of Time," p. 17.

NOTES - CHAPTER FIVE (continued)

32.   Carter Henderson, "The Future of Home Economics: A Deliberately Unorthodox View" (Speech at Florida State University, March 1978). The author quotes data published by the Worldwatch Institute.

33.   Statistics Canada, *Household Facilities by Income and Other Characteristics, 1980* (Ottawa: Supply and Services Canada, 1981). The following data in the text on household facilities also come from this volume.

34.   Statistics Canada, *National Income and Expenditure Accounts, Fourth Quarter, 1981* (Ottawa: Supply and Services Canada, 1982).

35.   S. Burns, *Home Inc.* (Garden City: Doubleday & Co., 1975), p. 52.

36.   J. Gershuny, *After Industrial Society? The Emerging Self-Service Economy* (London: MacMillan & Co., 1978). Data from p. 78.

37.   For example, see: "Exploring the Underground Economy," *The Economist,* September 22, 1979; "The Underground Economy," *U.S. News and World Report,* October 22, 1979; "Underground Economy May Upset Ottawa's Plans," *Financial Post,* October 6, 1979; "The Underground Economy," *Saturday Night,* June 1980; "The Underground Economy's Hidden Force," *Business Week,* April 5, 1982; and "Hidden Economy Worth $54 Billion Defies Tax Man," *Globe and Mail,* April 24, 1982.

38.   See the articles by Edgar Feige, "How Big Is the Irregular Economy," and Peter Gutmann, "Statistical Illusions, Mistaken Policies," in *Challenge* (November/December 1979): 14-17 and 5-13. For a Canadian estimate, see R. Mirus and R. Smith, "Canada's Irregular Economy," *Canadian Public Policy* 7 (Summer 1981): 444-453. These and other studies are summarized in Vito Tanzi, *The Underground Economy in the United States and Abroad* (Lexington, Mass.: Lexington Books, 1982).

CHAPTER SIX
POLICY IMPLICATIONS

1. Statistics Canada, *National Income and Expenditure Accounts,* vol. 3 (Ottawa: Information Canada, 1975).

2. Robert Lekachman, *Economists at Bay* (New York: McGraw-Hill Co., 1976), p. 119.

3. Ibid., p. 117.

4. For a particularly thought-provoking discussion of this issue, see Ivan Illich, *Shadow Work* (Boston: Marion Boyars Publishers, 1981).

5. Betty Friedan, *The Second Stage* (New York: Summit Books, 1982).

6. P.J. Usher, *Renewable Resources in the Future of Northern Labrador* (Nain: Labrador Inuit Association, 1982).

APPENDIX A
HOW ECONOMISTS VIEW LIFE

1. Paul Samuelson and Anthony Scott, *Economics,* 5th Canadian ed. (Toronto: McGraw-Hill Ryerson, 1980).

2. Gordon Boreham and Richard Leftwich, *Economic Thinking in a Canadian Context* (New York: Holt Rinehart & Winston, 1971).

3. Richard T. Ely, *An Introduction to Political Economy* (New York: Hunt & Eaton, 1893), p. 22.

4. Ibid., pp. 23-24.

5. F.W. Taussig, *Principles of Economics,* vol. 1 (New York:

NOTES - APPENDIX A (continued)

Macmillan Co., 1913), p. 19.

6. Ibid., Chapter 59.

7. Sumner Slichter, *Modern Economic Society* (New York: Henry Holt & Co., 1931), p. 113.

8. Ibid., p. 562.

9. Ibid., pp. 562-563.

10. Paul A. Samuelson, *Economics,* 4th ed. (New York: McGraw-Hill, 1958), p. 168.

11. J.M. Clark, *The Economics of Overhead Costs* (Chicago: University of Chicago Press, 1923).

12. Ibid., pp. 354-355.

13. Margaret Reid, *Economics of Household Production* (New York: John Wiley & Sons, 1934).

14. Ibid., pp. v and 3.

15. Thorstein Veblen, *The Theory of the Leisure Class* (New York: Macmillan Co., 1899). For a good short discussion of Veblen's work, see George Soule, *Ideas of the Great Economists* (New York: New American Library, 1952), Chapter 8.

APPENDIX B
THE VILLAGE ECONOMY

1. This appendix is taken largely from P.J. Usher, "A Northern Perspective on the Informal Economy" (Ottawa: Perspective

NOTES - APPENDIX B (continued)

Series, Vanier Institute of the Family, 1980). For further reading, see M. Asch, "The Dene Economy" in M. Watkins, ed., *Dene Nation: The Colony Within* (Toronto: University of Toronto Press, 1977), pp. 44-67; T.R. Berger, *Northern Frontier--Northern Homeland* (Report of the Mackenzie Valley Pipeline Inquiry), 2 vols. (Ottawa: Supply and Services Canada, 1977); R.T. Bowles, *Social Impact Assessment in Small Communities* (Toronto: Butterworth & Co., 1981); H. Brody, *Maps and Dreams* (Vancouver: Douglas & McIntyre, 1981); I. LaRusic, *Negotiating a Way of Life* and *Income Security for Subsistence Hunters* (Ottawa: Research Division, Department of Indian and Nothern Affairs, 1979 and 1982); M. Watkins, "From Underdevelopment to Development" in M. Watkins, ed., *Dene Nation* (loc. cit.), pp. 85-99; and R.J. Wolfe et al., *Subsistence-Based Economies in Coastal Communities of Southwest Alaska* (Technical Paper no. 89) (Juneau: Division of Subsistence, Alaska Department of Fish and Game, 1984).

2. See note 14 under Chapter Five.

3. For some analogies in the urban informal economy, see P. Armstrong, *Labour Pains: Women's Work in Crisis* (Toronto: Women's Educational Press, 1984), especially Chapter 5, "Household Labour."

BIBLIOGRAPHY

(The following references are in addition to those cited in the Notes.)

BOOKS

Andrew, Ed, *Closing the Iron Cage: The Scientific Management of Work and Leisure.* (Montreal: Black Rose Books, 1981).

Applegath, John, *Working Free: Practical Alternatives to the 9-to-5 Job* (New York: Amacom, 1982).

Berk, Sarah, ed., *Women and Household Labor* (Beverly Hills: Sage Publications, 1980).

Blaxall, M. and Reagan, B., eds., *Women and the Work Place* (Chicago: University of Chicago Press, 1976).

Bowles, S., Gordon, D. and Weisskopf, T., *Beyond the Waste Land: A Democratic Alternative to Economic Decline* (Garden City: Anchor Press, 1983).

The Briarpatch Book (San Francisco/Danbury, N.H.: New Glide/ Reed of Addison House, 1978).

Campfens, Hubert, ed., *Rethinking Community Development in a Changing Society* (Guelph: Ontario Community Development Society, 1983).

Co-operative Union of Canada, *A Co-operative Development Strategy for Canada* (Report of the National Task Force

167

Co-operative Development) (Ottawa: CUC, 1984).

Daly, Herman, *Steady-State Economics* (San Francisco: W.H. Freeman & Co., 1977).

Degler, Carl, *At Odds: Women and the Family in America* (Don Mills, Ont.: Oxford University Press, 1980).

Employment and Immigration Canada, *Community Economic Development in Rural Canada* (Ottawa: Supply and Services Canada, 1981).

Ferguson, Marilyn, *The Aquarian Conspiracy* (Los Angeles: Jeremy P. Tarcher, 1980).

Friedman, R. and Schweke, W., eds., *Expanding the Opportunity to Produce* (Washington: Corporation for Enterprise Development, 1981).

Handy, Charles, *The Future of Work* (New York: Basil Blackwell, 1984).

Harman, Willis, *An Incomplete Guide to the Future* (San Francisco: San Francisco Press, 1976).

Hawken, Paul, *The Next Economy* (New York: Holt, Rinehart & Winston, 1983).

Heilbroner, Robert, *The Making of Economic Society*, 2nd ed. (Englewood Cliffs, N.J.: Prentice-Hall, 1968).

_____, *The Worldly Philosophers* (New York: Simon & Schuster, 1953).

Henderson, Hazel, *Creating Alternative Futures: The End of Economics* (New York: Berkley Publishing, 1978).

_____, *The Politics of the Solar Age: Alternatives to Economics* (Garden City: Anchor Books, 1981).

Henry, Stuart, *The Hidden Economy* (Oxford: Oxford University Press, 1978).

Hirsch, Fred, *Social Limits to Growth* (Cambridge: Harvard University Press, 1976).

Illich, Ivan, *The Right to Useful Unemployment* (London: Marion Boyars Publishers, 1978).

Jackson, E.T., *Community Economic Self-Help and Small-Scale Fisheries* (Ottawa: Department of Fisheries and Oceans, 1984).

Johnson, Warren, *Muddling Toward Frugality* (Boulder, Colo.: Shambala Publications, 1978).

Kome, Penney, *Somebody Has to Do It: Whose Work Is Housework?* (Toronto: McClelland & Stewart, 1982).

Leibenstein, Harvey, *Beyond Economic Man* (Cambridge: Harvard University Press, 1976).

Leiss, William, *The Limits to Satisfaction* (Toronto: University of Toronto Press, 1967).

Lekachman, Robert, *Reaganomics: Greed Is Not Enough* (New York: Pantheon Books, 1982).

Lindblom, Charles, *Politics and Markets* (New York: Basic Books, 1977).

MacLeod, Greg, *It Can Be Done: Community Corporations that Work* (Ottawa: Canadian Council on Social Development, 1985).

Newland, K., *Productivity: The New Economic Context* (Washington: Worldwatch Institute, 1982).

OECD, *A Medium Term Strategy for Employment and Manpower Policies* (Paris: OECD, 1978).

Polanyi, Karl, *The Great Transformation* (Boston: Beacon Press, 1957).

Reich, Robert, *The Next American Frontier* (New York: Penguin Books, 1983).

Robertson, James, *The Sane Alternative* (London: James Robertson, 1978).

Sale, Kirkpatrick, *Human Scale* (New York: Coward, McCann & Geoghegan, 1980).

Schell, Jonathan, *The Fate of the Earth* (London: Pan Books, 1982).

Science Council of Canada, *Canada as a Conserver Society* (Ottawa: Science Council, 1977).

Shankland, Graeme, *Our Secret Economy* (London: Anglo-German Foundation, 1980).

Shegda, Ron, *The Regenerative Economy* (Medford, Maine: Friends for Community Development, 1984).

Skitovsky, Tibor, *The Joyless Economy* (Oxford: Oxford University Press, 1976).

Thompson, E.P., *The Making of the English Working Class* (Harmondsworth: Penguin Books, 1968).

Thurow, Lester, *Dangerous Currents: The State of Economics* (New York: Random House, 1983).

Tofler, Alvin, *The Third Wave* (New York: William Morrow & Co., 1980).

Wright, David, *Co-operatives and Community* (London: Bedford Square Press, 1979).

Zaretsky, Eli, *Capitalism, the Family, and Personal Life* (New York: Harper & Row, 1976).

ARTICLES, PROCEEDINGS, REPORTS

Bond, Jessie, "Back to Barter, Skills Exchange," *Communities,* no. 52 (February/March 1982): 5-9.

"Co-op America Catalog," *Communities,* no. 58 (April/May 1983): 17-48.

Dyson, William, "Canada and the Informal Economy" (Ottawa: Perspective Series, Vanier Institute of the Family, 1982).

"Economics and Work," *Communities,* no. 47 (February/March 1984): 22-31.

Gershuny, J., "The Informal Economy," *Futures* (February 1979): 3-15.

_____, and Pahl, R.E., "Britain in the Decade of the Three Economies," *New Society* (3 January 1980).

Glossop, Robert, "The Family and the Economy in the Decade of the 1980s" (Ottawa: Perspective Series, Vanier Institute of the Family, 1979).

Heinze, Rolf and Olk, Thomas, "Development of the Informal Economy: A Strategy for Resolving the Crisis of the Welfare State," *Futures* (June 1982): 189-204.

Huber, Joseph, "Social Ecology and Dual Economy," *International Federation for Development Alternatives Dossier,* no. 18 (July/ August 1980): 2-9.

Lane, Robert, "Markets and Politics: The Human Product," *British Journal of Political Science* 11, pt. I (January 1981): 1-16.

McRobie, George, "Towards a Sustainable Technology: Reflections on Appropriate Technology for Poor and Rich Countries" (Ottawa: Perspective Series, Vanier Institute of the Family, 1983).

Nicholls, William, "Strategies of Self-Reliance, Co-Reliance and Self-Sufficiency and Their Meaning for Rural Families"

(Ottawa: Perspective Series, Vanier Institute of the Family, 1981).

OECD, "The Economic and Social Role of Local Level Employment Initiatives" (Paris: OECD, February 1984).

Pahl, R.E., "Employment, Work and the Domestic Division of Labour," *International Journal of Urban and Regional Research* 4 (1980): 1-20.

_____, "Family, Community and Unemployment," *New Society* (21 January 1982).

Robertson, James, "Seeing Our Economy Whole: Satisfying Personal, Familial and Community Needs" (Ottawa: Vanier Institute of the Family, 1978).

Vanier Institute of the Family, *The Future of Work,* Proceedings of an International Seminar held at St. George's House, Windsor Castle, England, 1981.

_____, *Reshaping Development, 1984 and Beyond,* Proceedings of a Seminar held at St. Mary's University, Halifax, Nova Scotia, 1983.

_____, *Reshaping the Welfare State,* Proceedings of a Seminar held at the Couchiching Conference Centre, Ontario, 1982.

ABOUT THE AUTHORS

DAVID P. ROSS

David Ross, a social economist with graduate degrees from Alberta and Duke universities, has worked with the federal government cabinet office, the OECD in Paris, the Canadian Council on Social Development and the Vanier Institute of the Family. He has taught in the schools of economics, public administration and social work at Windsor, Ottawa, Carleton and McGill universities in Canada. His most recent publications are *The Canadian Fact Book on Income Distribution, The Working Poor* and *The Canadian Fact Book on Poverty*. He was a Canadian participant in the first international conference on the informal economy held in Rome in 1982 and The Other Economic Summit (TOES) held in London in 1985. Dr. Ross is now a social economics consultant and lecturer living in Ottawa.

PETER J. USHER

Peter Usher is a social scientist with graduate degrees in geography from McGill and the University of British Columbia. For over 20 years, he has undertaken research and consulting in northern Canada for the federal government and for several Native peoples' organizations. Dr. Usher is the author of numerous monographs and articles on problems of economic development and resource management in the North, and currently maintains an independent research and consulting practice in Ottawa.